MANGAJIN's
BASIC JAPANESE
through comics PART 2

MANGAJIN 's BASIC JAPANESE through comics PART 2

A compilation of 24 *Basic Japanese* columns
from *Mangajin* magazine

漫画人
MANGAJIN, Inc.
Marietta, Georgia

Cover by Ashizawa Kazuko

Distributed in the United States by Weatherhill, Inc.
41 Monroe Turnpike
Trumbull, Connecticut 06611

Distributed in Japan by Sekai Shuppan Kenkyu Center
2-18-9 Minami-Aoyama, Minato-ku
Tokyo 107

Published by Mangajin, Inc.
Box 7119, Marietta, Georgia 30065

Printed in the United States of America
First edition

ISBN 0-9634335-4-7

Contents / 目次

Introduction

In 1993 we published a compilation of the Basic Japanese columns from the first 24 issues of *Mangajin* magazine under the title *Basic Japanese Through Comics*. (See page 167 for a list of the topics covered in that volume.) Looking back on it now, we should have added Part 1 to that title, but at the time we were not completely convinced that there would ever be a Part 2. In fact, *Basic Japanese Through Comics* has been very warmly received by students and teachers, as well as by people who just have a casual interest in "picking up a little Japanese." So we now bring you Part 2, compiled from *Mangajin* issue Nos. 25–48.

If you're not familiar with *Mangajin* magazine, you can flip to page 164 for more information, but suffice it to say that *Mangajin* uses excerpts from authentic Japanese manga (created in Japan by Japanese artists and writers, for Japanese readers) to present the Japanese language as it is really spoken, and to give readers an inside view of contemporary Japanese society. In *Mangajin* magazine, most of the manga are presented as complete stories, rather than single-panel examples as in this book.

The name *Mangajin* is a play on two Japanese words, *manga* (漫画,"comics") and *jin* (人,"people"). It sounds like the English word "magazine" as rendered in Japanese—*magajin* (マガジン).

Manga may mean "comics," but in Japan they are serious business. Unlike American-style comics, manga are not just "kid stuff," but a highly developed medium for entertainment and education, popular among adults as well as children. It is estimated that manga account for over one third of all books and magazines published in Japan. Because they are so widely read, manga are as powerful as TV in shaping popular culture, and play an integral role in forming national attitudes, starting national fads, and shaping the national language in Japan.

In producing the Basic Japanese column, a particular word, phrase or concept is selected as a theme, and our team of "manga markers" goes through small mountains of manga books and periodicals searching for examples of that usage. The marked examples are reviewed by the editorial staff and examples are selected that 1) communicate the context and situation, 2) are visually interesting, 3) are typical or representative examples of actual usage. The examples are then organized into a flow or pattern, and the translation and annotation is done.

The Basic Japanese column has always been one of the most popular features of *Mangajin* magazine. Since the examples are "real" Japanese, some of the material is fairly advanced, but it is always made accessible even to beginners.

One of the more socially significant differences between English and Japanese is the existence of what can be called "politeness levels" in Japanese. These generally have no counterpart in English, so we use codes to indicate the level of politeness. This system is explained in detail on page 10.

We also provide a pronunciation guide on page 11, but if you ever intend to actually speak any of the material presented here, you'll probably require some additional help, preferably from a live, qualified teacher.

Mangajin magazine is found in select bookstores or can be ordered by calling 1-800-552-3206.

Acknowledgments:

This book includes material from the publishers Shogakukan, Kodansha, Take Shobo, Chuo Koronsha, Futabasha, Shueisha, and others. The publishing business in Japan is very competitive, and these companies have a long history of rivalry. We thank them for cooperating in this project and allowing us to combine their material in one volume. In conjunction with the matter of copyrights and permissions, we thank Moteki Hiromichi, the head of Sekai Shuppan Kenkyu Center (*Mangajin*'s representative in Japan) for his efforts in securing permission from these publishers.

The people who originally created these lessons for *Mangajin* magazine include Wayne Lammers, Lev Grote, Ben Beishline, Vaughan P. Simmons, Laura Silverman, Virginia Murray, Ashizawa Kazuko, and Okuyama Ikuko. Compilation of the material in this book was coordinated by Virginia Murray.

How to Learn Japanese
(without moving to Japan)

by Karen Yahara

No matter how diligent, motivated, and prepared you are, studying Japanese in the US requires a certain level of ingenuity. You simply will not be getting the daily, or hourly, reinforcement that you would get if you were studying in Japan, where you can "practice" pretty much just by being alive. But this does not mean that you have no chance of becoming proficient. If you are willing to go beyond the basic textbook approach and find creative ways to reinforce your studies, you'll find that your geographic disadvantage need not be insurmountable. And while participating in a structured class at some point is probably a good idea, there's plenty that you can do on your own.

The Basics

The first thing to realize is that the serious study of Japanese is not a cheap proposition, and you will not go far without assembling the basic language-learning tools. A Japanese-English dictionary, English-Japanese dictionary, and kanji dictionary are essential, and should be purchased early. When choosing, be sure to consider your current ability, and avoid any dictionary that you will not be able to fully utilize; in other words, don't waste your money on the biggest dictionary you can find if it will be of no use for the first two or three years.

Once you've assembled your dictionaries, you will need a textbook to act as a base for your studies. There are literally hundreds of Japanese textbooks available these days, and it is easy to be overwhelmed when it comes time to choose. At the outset, you must decide between a text that uses romanization and one that jumps right in with the kana syllabaries. (If you plan to study Japanese long-term, you may as well master the writing system as soon as possible.) Also, some texts are geared for self-study while others are more conducive to classroom use, so choose carefully.

Finally, you will probably want to get a set of tapes—preferably, tapes that go with the textbook you have selected. Listen to them carefully and listen to them often, but realize that the language you hear is purely for consumption by non-native students of the language. When you're ready to learn the language as it's really used, consider the options below.

Video Language

Because you will be studying in Boise or Austin, and not in downtown Yokohama, your exposure to the language will obviously be limited to the time you spend actively studying.

One way to complement the time you spend with your text is to rent videos of Japanese television shows. If you live in or near a town with any sizable Japanese population, there will most likely be a store that carries Japanese videos for rent. Ask a clerk to point you in the direction of the most insipid soap opera or evening drama that they have on the shelves.

While lacking in dramatic value, these shows are excellent for the beginning language student; featuring "real" people in "everyday" situations, they are full of practical and usable language.

When you watch, have your J-E dictionary and a notebook at your side, and be ready to stop and repeat sections frequently. You will at times be thwarted by colloquial expressions that you can't possibly recognize, but don't be discouraged: the combination of context, familiar vocabulary, and your handy dictionary should allow you to decipher a large portion of the dialog. When you reach the point where you're able to understand a fair percentage of what is being said, start to concentrate on the characters' intonation and work on making your own spoken Japanese sound more natural.

(For more advanced students, books-on-tape are another option for improving listening comprehension and pronunciation skills.)

Ways Around the Kanji Wall

There are as many methods for kanji mastery as there are gaijin trying to master it. The key lies in finding the method that works best for you.

If you are a visually oriented learner, you may do best relying on mnemonic devices to memorize the characters. Several creative texts, including *Kanji Pict-o-Graphix* and *Kanji Isn't That Hard*, are available to provide useful examples. But if these picture/story combinations only confuse things, you may be better off following a more strict memorization routine. This can include a combination of flashcards, *genkō yōshi*, and written repetition. *Genkō yōshi*, the graph paper-like sheets used for handwritten reports in Japan, are helpful in that they force you to concentrate on character balance when you write.

No matter what your method, mastering kanji means just one thing: practice. Once you've memorized the first 100 to 200 characters, the best thing to do is to begin reading Japanese children's books. The grammar will be simple, the vocabulary limited, and the script primarily kana and simple kanji. A series like *Kodansha's Nihongo Folktales* is especially useful because it contains basic English translations and cultural notes.

A Lot Between the Covers

Japanese magazines are another surprisingly effective study tool for students at almost any level, including beginners, since the majority of Japanese advertisements consist almost solely of imported words in katakana. Use the photos or illustrations in the ads as clues, and try to decipher the strange semi-English words being used to sell everything from fashion to household cleaning products.

If you've already conquered a fair number of kanji, buy a magazine that focuses on a subject you're interested in (sports, fashion, photography, etc.) and use it to learn vocabulary in this field. If it's a subject you know well, you'll find that your knowledge and limited Japanese will carry you far. (Readers of *Mangajin* already know how useful the magazine method can be. There are also several bilingual magazines, including the *Hiragana Times* and a new publication called *Turn*, that can make magazine reading a learning experience.)

Kid Stuff

There is a lot to be said for learning a language the way children do. Japan, a notoriously study-intensive country, has a multitude of kanji drillbooks and study guides available for its youngsters.

There are several excellent drillbook series, the most well known being the one created by Kumon, the "cram school" kings. The series is broken down by grade, so you can find the level that suits your current abilities and work your way through the entire series. In the first-grade kanji book, to give an example, students are drilled on 80 characters through a combination of quizzes, games, and writing practice exercises. The answers appear in the back of the book, so you can check your own work.

Making Progress?

Once you've spent some time studying on your own, you may begin to wonder where you stand. A good diagnostic tool is the Japanese Language Proficiency Test. The test, which in North America is administered in Los Angeles, Chicago, New York, and Vancouver, covers grammar, vocabulary, reading comprehension, kanji recognition, and listening comprehension.

Even if you don't want to take the test, just going through the preparation books can help you polish your skills in these areas, and also give you a good feel for your various strengths and weaknesses. If you do decide to take the test, and pass level one, you are ready to enter a Japanese university!

———————

Karen Yahara is the owner of Sasuga Japanese Bookstore in Boston.

(The kanji characters shown at left read Nihongo, *"Japanese language"; shown above,* dokugaku, *"self-study.")*

WARNING!

Some people say there are few true "cusswords" in Japanese because it's possible to be just as offensive by using a lower politeness level.

The politeness levels found in Japanese frequently have no counterpart in English. This can cause problems for translators. The words *suru* and *shimasu* would both be rendered simply as "do" in English, but in Japanese there is a very clear distinction between the "politeness" levels of these two words. In a more extreme case, *shiyagaru* would also be translated simply as "do" in English, but in Japanese this word is openly offensive.

Learning Japanese from *manga* is a good way to get a "feel" for these politeness levels. You see words used in the context of a social setting.

The danger in "picking up" Japanese is that even though most Japanese people appreciate the fact that you are interested in learning their language and will make allowances because you are a beginner, misused politeness levels can be pretty grating on the Japanese ear, even if they do not reach the point of being truly offensive.

How can I be safe? Politeness Level 3 can be used in almost any situation. Although it might not be completely natural in a very formal situation, it will not cause offense. If you want to be safe, use PL2 only with friends and avoid PL1 altogether.

"Politeness Level" Codes used in this book

(PL4) **Politeness Level 4: Very Polite**
Typically uses special honorific or humble words, such as *nasaimasu* or *itashimasu*.

(PL3) **Politeness Level 3: Ordinary Polite**
Typified by the verb *desu*, or the *-masu* ending on other verbs.

(PL2) **Politeness Level 2: Plain / Abrupt**
For informal conversation with peers.
• "dictionary form" of verbs
• adjectives without *desu*

(PL1) **Politeness Level 1: Rude / Condescending**
Typified by special words or verb endings, usually not "obscene" in the Western sense of the word, but equally insulting.

These levels are only approximations: To simplify matters, we use the word "politeness," although there are actually several dimensions involved (formality, deference, humility, refinement, etc.). While the level of respect (or lack of it) for the person spoken to or spoken about can determine which words are used, verb forms are determined largely by the formality of the situation. Thus, it is difficult to label the verb *irassharu* (the informal form of an honorific verb) using this simple four-level system. In such cases we sometimes use combined tags, such as (PL4-3).

Rather than trying to develop an elaborate system which might be so confusing as to actually defeat the purpose, we feel that this system, even with its compromises, is the best way to save our readers from embarrassing situations.

Pronunciation Guide

> **This is only a guide!** *Japanese pronunciation is relatively straightforward, but if you don't want to sound like a gaijin, you'll probably have to make some adjustments in your basic speech habits—hard to do without external feedback. We strongly recommend getting help from a qualified instructor.*

Pronunciation is probably one of the easier aspects of Japanese. Vowel sounds don't vary as they do in English. While English uses the five letters a, e, i, o, u to make 20 or so vowel sounds, in Japanese there are 5 vowels and 5 vowel sounds—the pronunciation is always constant. There are only a few sounds in the entire phonetic system which will be completely new to the speaker of English.

The five vowels in Japanese are written *a, i, u, e, o* in *rōmaji* (English letters). This is also the order in which they appear in the Japanese kana "alphabet." They are pronounced:

a   like the *a* in f*a*ther, or h*a* h*a*!
i   like the *i* in macaron*i*
u   like the *u* in Z*u*lu
e   like the *e* in g*e*t, or *e*xtra
o   like the *o* in s*o*lo

The length of time that a vowel sound is held or sustained makes it "long" or "short" in Japanese. Don't confuse this with what are called long or short vowels in English. The long vowel in Japanese has exactly the same pronunciation as the short vowel, but it's held for twice as long. Long vowels are designated by a line over the vowel (*dōmo, okāsan*), or by repeating the vowel (*iimasu*).

The vowels i and u are sometimes not fully sounded (as in the verb *desu* or the verb ending *-mashita*). This varies between individual speakers and there are no fixed rules.

Japanese consonant sounds are pretty close to those of English. The notable exception is the r sound, which is like a combination of the English r and l, winding up close to the d sound. If you say the name Eddy and touch the tip of your tongue lightly behind the upper front teeth, you have an approximation of the Japanese word *eri* (collar).

Doubled consonants are pronounced by pausing just slightly after the sound is formed, and then almost "spitting out" the rest of the word. Although this phenomenon does not really occur in English, it is somewhat similar to the k sound in the word bookkeeper.

The *n* sound: When it is not attached to a vowel (as in *na, ni, nu, ne, no*), *n* is like a syllable in itself, and as such it receives a full "beat." When *n* is followed by a vowel to which it is not attached, we mark it with an apostrophe. Note the difference between the word for "no smoking," *kin'en* (actually four syllables: *ki-n-e-n*), and the word for "anniversary," *kinen* (three syllables: *ki-ne-n*).

The distinctive sound of spoken Japanese is partly due to the even stress or accent given to each syllable. This is one reason why pronunciation of Japanese is relatively easy. Although changes of pitch do occur in Japanese, in most cases these are not essential to the meaning. Beginners, especially Americans, are probably better off to try for flat, even intonation. Rising pitch for questions and stressing words for emphasis are much the same as in English.

Illustration by Anthony Owsley

APOLOGY
From the translators

Since most of the people who read *Basic Japanese Through Comics* and *Mangajin* are interested in the Japanese language, we strive to reflect the nature of the original Japanese in our translations, sometimes at the expense of smooth, natural-sounding English. We ask that you please give us your honorable acceptance of this fact.

– Trans.

BASIC JAPANESE through comics

Lesson 25 • Gestures & Body Language (I)

Non-verbal communication occurs in all cultures, but it seems to play an especially important role in Japan. This has been ascribed to the Japanese fondness for stylized gestures (as in *kabuki*), the fondness for transmitting ideas without resorting to direct speech (witness terms such as 以心伝心 *ishin denshin* or 腹芸 *haragei*), or a kind of distrust of words due to the ease with which they may be manipulated; but whatever the reasons, Japanese is rich in these non-verbal signals.

As a non-Japanese, you are especially likely to encounter these because of the somewhat illogical belief on the part of some Japanese people in the universality of "sign language." This alone is good reason to become familiar with them, but as Jack Seward points out in his book *Japanese In Action*, learning and using these gestures can also be an effective way to give the impression that you are deeply steeped in Japanese culture (should you care to give such an impression).

The visual nature of this kind of communication lends itself well to study through manga. Although our research did not turn up examples of every conceivable gesture, we found more than could be covered in one lesson, so here we present Part I of our lesson in Gestures and Body Language.

A sign of embarrassment

The hand to the back of the head (scratching optional) is a sign of embarrassment or puzzlement, and it gets heavy use in manga. Here Tabatake, not exactly a ladies' man, is inviting his librarian friend for a walk. He saw her with another man the day before, but he is hoping that he has a chance with her.

© Kubonouchi Eisaku / *Tsurumoku Dokushin-Ryō*, Shogakukan

Tabatake: ボ...ボク 今日 仕事 休み で さ。 ／ 来ちゃった.....
Bo... Boku kyō shigoto yasumi de sa. ／ *Kichatta.....*
I/me today work/job rest/day off is (and) (emph.) came
"I . . . I have today off, you know, (so) ／ I just came by . . . ." (PL2)

* the particle *de* acts as a continuing form of the verb *desu*.
* *kichatta* is a contraction of *kite shimatta*. The *-te* form of a verb plus *shimau* means to do completely, and often implies, "went ahead and ～"

Indicating yourself

To refer to themselves, Japanese people point to their nose instead of their heart. In this scene from *Be-Bop High School*, a rather large and tough-looking girl has just informed two boys that they are going to pay for making fun of her name, but Hiroshi feels he should be let off the hook.

© Kiuchi Kazuhiro / *Be-Bop High School,* Kodansha

Hiroshi: え？ ／ 俺 も？
E? / *Ore mo?*
huh I/me also
"Huh? Me too?" (PL2)

- *ore* is a rough, masculine word for I/me.
- the girl's name is 妙子 (Taeko), and the kanji 妙 (which actually means "clever/admirable," or sometimes "mysterious") is made up of the two radicals *onna* ("woman/female") and *suku(nai)* ("a small quantity/lacking"). The boys laughingly commented that her parents should be commended for giving her such an appropriate name, since she is so lacking in femininity.

Five rival girls have just been chosen to represent Japan in Olympic judo. A reporter has just asked how they feel about being selected, and Sayaka, the rich and arrogant "bad girl" of the story, is talking about the gold medal she expects to bring back.

© Urasawa Naoki / *Yawara!,* Shogakukan

Sayaka: 金メダル が 似合う 女王らしい 人 って、 そう は いません もの!!
Kin medaru ga niau joōrashii hito tte, sō wa imasen mono!!
gold medal (subj.) become/suit queen-like person (quote) so many as for not exist (explan.)
"There aren't that many queen-like women that a gold medal would be becoming to!!" (PL3)

Sound FX: ホーホッホッホ
Hō ho! ho! ho
(effect of a feminine laugh)

Yuki : ここ に いる わ、 ここに!!
Koko ni iru wa, koko ni!!
here at exists (fem. colloq.) here at
"Here, there's one right here!" (PL2)

Come here

Extending the arm, bending the wrist to angle the hand down a bit, and then waving the fingers is the sign for "come here" in Japan. The similarity of this gesture to the western "good-bye" wave can be a source of confusion in culturally mixed company.

In this example, Yowatari-kun has just transferred from another school, and is introducing himself to his new classmates. His attempts to impress them don't seem to be working, and his teacher is calling him back to his seat.

© Kubo Kiriko / *Imadoki no Kodomo,* Shogakukan

Yowatari-kun: おかしい な... 受けない。
Okashii na ... ukenai.
strange (colloq.) isn't well received
"That's odd . . . They're not impressed." (PL2)

Teacher: 世渡君、 自己紹介 は そのくらい にして、
Yowatari-kun, jiko shōkai wa sono kurai ni shite,
(name) self-introduction as for about that much make/leave at

席 に 着きなさい。
seki ni tsukinasai.
seat to arrive
"Yowatari-kun, leave your introduction at that and come to your seat, please." (PL3)

- *ukenai,* is from the verb *ukeru,* which, in addition to its primary meaning of "receive," is used to mean "be popular/be well received/appeal (to the public)."
- when referring to a seat, the verb *tsuku* means "sit/take a place at."

The yakuza ("gangster") in this scene has just bribed some people to leave their seats so that he and his new friends can enjoy a good view of the horse race they have bet on. Here we see a front view of the "come here" gesture.

© Ōtsuba Maki / *Sūpā Kotobuki Kawazaki Ten 1•2 no 3K,* Futabasha

Yakuza: ほーら、 こっち こっち
Hōra, kotchi kotchi
hey here here
"Hey, over here, over here." (PL2)

親切な 人 が 席 を
Shinsetsu na hito ga seki o
kind person (subj.) seat (obj.)

ゆずって くれた ぞ。
yuzutte kureta zo.
give/offer (favor) (masc. emph.)
"Some kind people have given us their seats" (PL2)

- *hora,* in this case elongated to *hōra,* is a word used to get someone's attention, and has the feel of, "look" or "hey."
- *yuzutte* is the *-te* form of the verb *yuzuru* ("offer/yield/give [up] to someone else").
- *zo* is a rough masculine emphatic ending.

The negative response/Just saying "no"

Declining an offer or saying "no" is often accompanied by waving a hand back and forth in front of the face. This is the gesture of choice for non-English-speaking Japanese people when approached by a foreigner that they assume doesn't speak Japanese.

In this example, Yawara has gone to a disco for the first time, and some of her friends are trying to get her to come out and dance, but she hasn't worked up the courage to hit the floor yet.

© Urasawa Naoki / *Yawara!*, Shogakukan

Sound FX: ドダン
Dodan
(effect of loud [disco] music in the background)

Yawara: あ...いえ、あたし達 まだ いい です....
A... ie,   atashitachi mada   ii   desu....
ah, no   we   still OK/good is/are
"Uh, no, we're not quite ready yet." (PL3)

ねっ、 富士子さん!
Ne!   Fujiko-san!
right/correct (name)
"Right, Fujiko?" (PL3)

- *atashi* is a feminine equivalent of *watashi*, ("I/me").

Yamamoto has been waiting for Kuwada to show up for a meeting, and is a bit miffed to see him approaching through the garden at a leisurely pace. When Kuwada makes his entrance, Yamamoto keeps his temper in check.

© Mōri & Uoto / *Kasai no Hito*, Shogakukan

Kuwada: どーも!   待ちました か?
Dōmo!   Machimashita ka?
thanks/well/sorry   waited   (?)
"Sorry, did you have to wait?" (PL3)

Yamamoto: いいえ! ちーっとも!!
Iie!   Chi–ttomo!!
no   not at all
"No, not in the least!"

なんも だー
Nanmo dā
not at all is
"Not at all." (PL2)

- *dōmo* spans a wide range of meanings, from "very" to "thank you" to "excuse me." (See Basic Japanese No. 8.)
- *chittomo* followed by a negative form means "not even a little . . ." The negative form of the verb *matsu* ("wait") is simply implied here. Yamamoto lengthens *chittomo* for emphasis.
- *nanmo* is used to mean "not at all," and essentially implies *nanimo sonna koto wa arimasen*. *Da* is sometimes added as an informal/colloquial touch.

The "OK" sign

The familiar signal for "OK" is also used in Japan, although it is a relatively recent import and more likely to be used by young people. Here Tabatake, an unrefined sort with a flair for the dramatic, has just offered his date a rose and his love. She thinks he is making a joke.

© Kubonouchi Eisaku / *Tsurumoku Dokushin-Ryō*, Shogakukan

Yayoi: はー...おっかしい!
Ha–... okkashii!
ah   funny
"Oh, that was funny!" (PL2)

Yayoi: 今 の ギャグ。ぐ よ。ぐ!
Ima no gyagu. Gu yo. Gu!
now 's gag   good (emph.) good   (PL2)
"That was a good gag. Good!" (PL2)

Tabatake: ギャ...ギャグ?
Gya ... Gyagu?
"G-gag?" (PL2?)

- *okashii* means "funny/hilarious." She adds emphasis by saying *okkashii.*
- *gyagu* is the katakana rendering of "gag."
- *gu* is taken from the English word "good."

Money

The older and more traditional meaning of the same sign is "money." Context will usually make this distinction clear. In this scene, a woman is asking someone how much he won gambling.

© Hosono / *Mama*, Shogakukan

なんぼ 勝った?
Nanbo katta?
how much won
"How much did you win?" (PL2)

- *nanbo* is dialect for "how much (money)."

Drinking

Altering the form of the OK/money gesture so that the thumb and index finger are open and the other fingers are curled in, and then giving a tipping motion is a reference to drinking. This gesture is taken from the shape of a small sake cup, but can refer to partaking of any kind of alcoholic beverage.

Kakarichō: ちょっと 一杯 やってかねえか、
Chotto ippai yattekanēka,
a little one cup won't (you) do-and-go
おごる ぞ。
ogoru zo.
treat   (masc emph.)
"Wanna stop for a drink on the way home? It's on me." (PL2)

Woman: へっ!!
He!
"What?" (PL2)

© Hayashi & Takai / *Yamaguchi Roppeita*, Shogakukan

- *yattekanē ka* is a rough/masculine contraction of *yatte ikanai ka*, from the *-te* form of *yaru* ("do") and the plain/abrupt negative of *iku* ("go").

Insulting gestures

A circling motion with the forefinger around the ear or temple indicates that the one referred to may not have both oars in the water. Strictly speaking, the motion should be counter-clockwise, since the term *hidari maki* (literally, "left winding" → "counter-clockwise") is used to mean "crazy/a screwball," or "eccentric," but in practice, any kind of circular motion will convey the meaning.

　　The family in this example is trying to develop their son's aesthetic sensibilities by having him listen to classical music and look at pictures of masterpieces of art, but it seems to be lost on him.

© Kubo Kiriko / *Imadoki no Kodomo*, Shogakukan

Mother: どう だった?
Dō　datta?
how　was
"How'd it go?" (PL2)

Sister: わかんない　だって。
Wakannai　datte.
doesn't understand　(quote)

あの 子 ダメ なん じゃなーい?
Ano　ko　dame　nan　ja na-i?
that child no good (explan.) isn't (he)
"He says he doesn't get it. Looks like he's hopeless." (PL2)

• *wakannai* is a contraction of *wakaranai*, the plain/abrupt past negative of *wakaru* ("understand").

"Akanbē"

Pulling down one eyelid to show the red of the eye, a gesture called *akanbē,* is something like the "moose antlers" sign in the U.S. The gesturer can say the full *akanbē,* or shorten it to simply *bē,* and sticking out the tongue is an optional finishing touch.

Miyuki: 正太 の バカ!!
Shōta　no　baka!!
(name) 's　idiot
"Shōta, you idiot!" (PL1)
べーだ
Bēda
(The noise accompanying the gesture)

© Kubonouchi Eisaku / *Tsurumoku Dokushin-Ryō*, Shogakukan

BASIC JAPANESE through comics

Lesson 26 • Gestures & Body Language (II)

In the last lesson, we introduced some of Japan's non-verbal communication signals, but there was too much material for one chapter. Although still not exhaustive, here is Part II.

The "V" sign

© Takahashi Rumiko / *Ranma 1/2*, Shogakukan

The "V for victory" sign apparently came to Japan first through the well-known photograph of Churchill (after WWII). In the 60s and 70s, however, it began to be used as the "peace" sign. It's now a kind of standard gesture for photos and poses in general, although it does retain some of the "victory" nuance (see the last illustration below).

In this example from *Ranma 1/2*, Ranma had been followed by an adversary trying to discover a weakness to exploit. Although the rival's aim was stealth, Ranma knew that he was being photographed, and made sure to strike a pose every time his picture was taken.

Posing for a picture is not the only occasion for the "V" sign. It is also used to indicate a sense of accomplishment, satisfaction, or happiness. Here a young restaurant worker is being told by the master chef that the food he prepared is satisfactory. He finds out in the next frame that the chef actually wanted food that didn't taste too good, so his accomplishment is questionable.

© Abe & Kurata / *Aji Ichimonme*, Shogakukan

Chef: ええ　　やろ。
Ē　　yaro.
good/fine　is/probably is
"It's fine" (PL2)

Ihashi: やった!
Yatta!
did (it)
"All right!" (PL2)

- *ē* is a dialect version of *ii,* ("good"), and *yaro* is Kansai dialect for *darō* ("is/probably").
- *yatta* is literally, "did (it)," but also carries the meaning of, "great/all right!" (See Basic Japanese 13)

Maru/Batsu

Something like "thumbs up/thumbs down," *maru* (◯) and *batsu* (✕) are used in Japanese schools when grading tests. (◯="good/correct"; ✕ ="no good/incorrect"; △[*sankaku*] ="partially correct") As the following scenes from *Aji Ichimonme* illustrate, they are also used as signs of approval/disapproval.

A restaurant critic who has his own TV show samples meals from various restaurants and gives his evaluation in the form of a *maru* or *batsu*. Restaurants blessed with a *maru* are swamped with business, while those given a *batsu* might as well close shop. In this first scene, a cook is talking about the show with a friend, and imitating the critic's gesture.

© Abe & Kurata / *Aji Ichimonme,* Shogakukan

Cook: マルーウって
Marū   tte
circle/pass (quote)
"When he says, 'maru' . . ." (PL2)

- he has lengthened the word *maru* for emphasis.

Here is the critic himself in action on his TV show.

Critic: バーツ!
Bātsu!
fail/no good
"Thumbs down!" (PL2)

FX: ガックリ
Gakkuri
(effect of being disappointed)

- *batsu* is lengthened, again for emphasis.

© Abe & Kurata / *Aji Ichimonme,* Shogakukan

The word *peke* is sometimes used as a synonym of *batsu*. The workers here are discussing the rating another restaurant was given.

© Abe & Kurata / *Aji Ichimonme,* Shogakukan

Ihashi: ペケ?
Peke?
no good/fail
"(It was given a) 'No good'?"
(PL2)

Leave it to me

Pounding your chest with one fist indicates confidence in your ability to do something, and is a way of assuring others that you will carry out your duties properly. Here Yamamoto has volunteered to treat his co-workers to some cherries. This may not seem like cause for chest-pounding, but it is early in the season and a small basket of cherries sells for ¥20,000.

Yamamoto: 任せて　下さい!!
Makasete　kudasai!!
leave to/entrust　please
"Leave it to me!" (PL3)

© Mōri & Uoto / *Kasai no Hito*, Shogakukan

The thumbs-up sign is used in Japan and carries pretty much the same meaning as in the West, i.e. "OK/good/understood/gotcha." In this scene, a small boy has just advised Shōta not to let Miyuki (Shōta's girlfriend) get away.

© Kubonouchi Eisaku / *Tsurumoku Dokushin-Ryō*, Shogakukan

Shōta: ああ... / 任せとけ!
Ā... / Makasetoke!
yeah　　　leave/entrust
"OK, I'll take care of it!"
(PL2)

• *makasetoke*, is a contraction of *makasete oke*, combining the *-te* form of *makaseru* ("leave/entrust") with the abrupt command form of *oku*. This use of *oku* implies that an action is made ("leaving it to me"), and left "as-is" — there is no need for further concern.

A show of strength

This gesture may look familiar, but the meaning in Japan is quite different. It is made without the vigorous movement that accompanies its obscene counterpart, and means that you are strong or skillful at something. The hand on the arm is to stress the flexed bicep. Here, Kuriko is pleased to have built a snowman on the patio of her apartment.

© Terashima Reiko / *Kuriko-san, Konnichi-wa*, Take Shobō

Husband: ベランダ　２つ分　の　雪　か
Beranda   futatsu-bun no yuki ka?
veranda/patio two portions of snow (?)
"The snow from two patios, huh?" (PL2)

Kuriko: 近所　　　　で　一番　大きい　雪ダルマ!
Kinjo   de ichiban ōkii   yuki daruma!
neighborhood at/in #1/most big   snowman
"It's the biggest snowman in the neighborhood!"
(PL2)

• *futatsu-bun* means "two portions," so *beranda futatsu-bun no yuki* means "two veranda portions of snow," or "the snow from two verandas."

• a snowman is not *yukiotoko* (or *yukihito*) in Japanese, but rather *yukidaruma* or "snow Daruma." Daruma is the Japanese name for Bodhidharma, who founded Zen Buddhism in China. Legend has it that he meditated for so long in one position that his arms and legs fell off. Daruma dolls, used in Japan as symbols of perseverance or charms for the fulfillment of various wishes, have a rounded shape with no arms or legs.

Catching goldfish from a pool of water with a scoop made of tissue paper is a common carnival game in Japan. Because the scoop is very flimsy and disintegrates almost as soon as it gets wet, the game requires considerable skill. The mother in this scene vows to go get a goldfish for her sick son, since he can't go to the nearby *matsuri* ("festival").

© Hosono / *Mama*, Shogakukan

Mother: そうだ、ママ　が　金魚　とってきて
Sō da,   mama ga kingyo totte kite
that's right mama (subj.) goldfish take and come

あげよっか?／うまい　ん　だ　ぞー。
ageyokka? / umai   n   da   zō.
(favor) (?)   skillful (explan.) is/am (masc. emph.)
**"I know! Should I go and get you a goldfish? /
I'm good at it, you know!"** (PL3)

Child: ううん。
U-un.
no
"Uh-uh!"

• using the *-te kuru* form of a verb (as in *totte kuru*) indicates that one intends to go do the action and then return to their present location.

• *ageyokka* is a colloquial form of *ageyō ka* ("should I give to/do for you?")

• *zo* is a rough/masculine particle for emphasis, but female speakers can use it for special effect in informal situations such as talking to kids (especially boys), among close friends, or when speaking to themselves.

Imploring

Putting the hands together with the fingers pointed up is a gesture used when worshipping or praying, and therefore relates to imploring or asking a favor. In this scene from *Be-Bop High School*, the devious Junko is asking her new "boyfriend" to call her by a pet name. He doesn't realize that she is setting him up as the butt of a joke.

© Kiuchi Kazuhiro / *Be-Bop Highschool*, Kodansha

Junko: おネがい! ね? 一度 だけ でも。 ねっねっ?
Onegai! Ne? Ichido dake demo. Ne! Ne!
please OK one time only even OK OK
"Please! OK? Even just once. Please, please?"
(PL2)

© Saimon Fumi / *Dōkyūsei*, Shogakukan

Kamoi has been asked by his old classmate Sawaguchi to come and cheer up a mutual friend of theirs. He sticks his foot in his mouth and makes the girl feel worse, so now he is pleading forgiveness.

Thanks

Kamoi: ゴメン!
Gomen!
sorry
"I'm sorry (forgive me)!" (PL2)

Giving thanks

The same gesture can be used as a "thank you." The man in this scene, a rich and famous gourmet, has just finished a simple but very well-made meal, the likes of which he hasn't had in some time.

© Kariya & Hanasaki/ *Oishinbo*, Shogakukan

Keikyoku: ごちそうさん。
Gochisōsan
"Thanks for the meal." (PL2)

- *gochisōsama* or *gochisōsan* is the standard expression used after finishing a meal. It doesn't lend itself well to translation, but definitely has the feeling of giving thanks for the food. People may say it even if they prepared the meal themselves and are eating alone. See Basic Japanese lesson No. 20.

Girlfriend/Mistress

The little finger, pointed straight up, is a sign referring to a man's love interest — girlfriend, mistress, even wife. To go along with the ambiguous nature of the gesture, the female in question is typically referred to simply as *kore* ("this"). The man in this scene is hiring a photographer to spy on his girlfriend because he suspects that she's been stepping out.

© Koike & Kagawa / *Suiito Rūmu* Shogakukan

Man: つまり　　わし の コレ。
Tsumari　　washi no kore.
in other words I/me 's "this"
"In a word, my *this* (mistress)." (PL2)

FX: びしっ
Bishi!
(effect of the impact of his outspokenness)

Senri: は . . . はァ . . .
Ha . . . hā . . .
"Y-yes sir. . ."

Man: 草川 ゆかり . . .　　24歳
Kusakawa Yukari . . .　　nijūyon-sai.
"Kusakawa Yukari; age twenty-four."

- *washi* is a version of *watashi/watakushi*, ("I/me") used by older males.

Even though the boss is paying, a coworker declines an invitation to go drinking after work, claiming that he has something he needs to take care of. Everyone thinks it a bit strange.

Mayumi: ひょっとして コレ じゃない?
Hyotto shite　　kore ja nai?
perhaps "this" isn't it
"By chance could it be *this*?"
(PL2)

© Hayashi & Takai / *Yamaguchi Roppeita*, Shogakukan

Sticky Fingers

The crooked forefinger is a reference to latching onto someone else's possessions. Here Hagure has stolen some medicine for a friend who can't afford it.

© Jōji Akiyama / *Haguregumo,* Shogakukan

Achiki: はい。／　でも　どうして　あなた　が　　　満月薬　　　を...
Hai. / Demo dōshite anata ga mangetsu-yaku o...
Yes. 　 but 　 why 　 you 　 (subj.) full-moon medicine (obj.)
"Yes. / But how did you get the full-moon medicine?" (PL2)

Hagure: これっ
Kore!
"'This' (I stole it)!"

- she is saying, "yes" to a question he asked her in the previous frame —whether she was taking the medicine secretly so the doctor wouldn't find out.
- she leaves her sentence incomplete, implying something like, "*Dōshite anata ga mangetsu-yaku o (motte-ita no desu ka)?*"

Putting dibs on something

You can stake your claim to something by licking your finger and then touching the object in question (or simply saying *Tsuba tsuketa*). This apparently originated as a way of claiming a piece of food. In this scene, Shōta has just been reunited with an acquaintance from his company training days, and she asks him if he has a girlfriend. When he says no, she reserves him for herself.

Sound FX: ぺろっ
Pero!
(effect of licking)

Nao-chan: ツバ　　つーけたっ!!
Tsuba tsūketa!!
saliva/spit attached
"I've got dibs on you!" (PL2)

Shōta: へ!?
He!?
"Huh?" (PL2)

- she lengthens the *tsu* in *tsuba* as a playful touch.

© Kubonouchi Eisaku / *Tsurumoku Dokushin-Ryō*

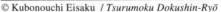

Lesson 27 • *Yappari / Yahari*

Certain words and phrases seem to give Japanese language students fits; no matter how many times they hear or look up the expression, they just can't get a feel for its real nuance. *Yappari* is one of these troublesome utterances, and it is used so often in Japanese speech that not being able to understand it can be very frustrating. The actual word is *yahari* (for kanji-heads, it can be written 矢張り, although the more common choice is hiragana, or occasionally katakana), but the colloquial *yappari* is more commonly used. Other informal variations include *yappashi*, and the minimal *yappa*.

One reason for the difficulty in understanding *yappari* is that it doesn't translate into a single cut-and-dried English phrase, but has a range of subtly different meanings. Perhaps the most basic use of *yappari* is to express confirmation of something you suspected or thought to be likely/true, or re-confirmation of something generally believed to be true.

But the best way to understand *yappari* is, *yappari*, to see it used in the context of some manga stories.

Really/After all

Kyū-san wakes up one morning to find that he has turned into a penguin. He heads off to work at the coffee shop, and although his co-worker complains about his turning on the air conditioning in December, no one around him seems to notice that he is a penguin. He wonders if it's just a hallucination caused by something he ate, but when he tries to pour a cup of coffee, he realizes that he really is a penguin.

© Tomisawa Chinatsu / *Katsushika Q*, Shogakukan

<u>Kyū-san</u>: だめ　だ!! /　やはり　ペンギン　だ!!
Dame da!! / Yahari pengin da!!
no good is　　　really/after all penguin am
"It's no use. I really am a penguin."
(PL2)

<u>Off panel</u>: あ～～あ
Ā–
(his co-worker's groan of dismay at
Kyū's spilling the coffee)

• *da* is the plain/abrupt form of *desu* ("is/
am/are").

Just as I suspected

There seems to be a curse on a certain artist's paintings. The artist himself died long ago in a mysterious fire, and now owners of his paintings are losing everything to strange fires also. Fujita suspects a scheme to get the owners to sell their paintings at low prices, and is trying to determine the cause of the original fire that killed the artist. Going through some old written records, he discovers evidence that the fire was an accident with an easily-explained cause.

© Hosano Fujihiko / *Gyararii Feiku*, Shogakukan

Fujita: これ だ！こいつ を 探していた の さ！
Kore da! Koitsu o sagashite-ita no sa!
this is this (obj.) was looking for (explan.)(emph.)
"This is it! This is what I was looking for!" (PL2)

やっぱり な、ふふふふ！
Yappari na, fu fu fu fu!
as expected (emph.) (laugh)
"Just as I suspected! Hee hee hee!" (PL2)

そうだろうと思った の さ、はははははは！
Sō darō to omotta no sa, ha ha ha ha ha!
is like that thought (explan.) (emph.) (laugh)
"I thought that was probably the case, Ha ha ha!" (PL2)

- *koitsu* is an expression for "this guy." Using it when referring to an object is slang.

At first these children think their father's card trick is "a miracle," but then they begin to suspect that it's just sleight of hand. Determined to figure out the secret of his trick, Hazuki pretends to sleep while Natsuki has him perform the trick again. Watching from behind, Hazuki catches him palming a card.

© Hoshisato Mochiru / *Tsuin Biinzu*, Shogakukan

Hazuki: ほら ほらなつきちゃん！
Hora hora Natsuki-chan!
look look name-(dimin.)
こげな とこ にカード、ほら！
koge-na toko ni kādo, hora!
that kind of place at card hey/see
"Look, look, Natsuki-chan! There's a card hidden here, see!" (PL2)

Natsuki: あーっ、やっぱり。
Ā! Yappari.
"Aha, just as we thought!" (PL2)

- *hora* is used to get someone's attention, like "look" or "hey."
- *-chan* is a diminutive equivalent of *-san* ("Mr./Ms.") used mostly with children and close friends.
- *koge-na* is dialect for *konna*, literally "this kind of," but used to imply "this (unexpected/strange) . . ."
- *toko* is short for *tokoro* ("place").
- Hazuki's sentence is left unfinished, implying *koge-na toko ni kādo (ga aru)*, lit. "(There's a) card in a place like this."

Speculations confirmed

© Hoshisato Mochiru / *Ribingu Gēmu*, Shogakukan

In this scene, the girl sitting down has been threatening to drop out of school. Izumi guesses that it's because she hates exams. The girl's reaction when confronted with this question confirms Izumi's suspicions.

Izumi:
もしかして　学校　が　いや　なんじゃなくて、
Moshi ka shite gakkō ga iya nan ja nakute,
perhaps　　　school　(subj.) disagreeable (explan.)　isn't

試験　が　いや　なん　じゃない?
shiken ga iya nan ja nai?
test(s) (subj.) disagreeable (explan.)　aren't
"Could it be that it's not school that you hate, it's the tests?" (PL2)

Sound FX: んぎくっ
nGiku!
(effect of being startled at having been found out)

Izumi: やっぱり。
Yappari.
"So that *is* it." (PL2)

- *moshi ka shite* is often used to begin a sentence that is speculation.
- the standard sound effect for being startled/shocked at something is *giku!* The initial *n* probably implies a cartoon-like, slightly delayed reaction.

After all

Mild-mannered Morris killed Michael and framed him for robbery in an attempt to get his inheritance: an English pub in which valuable Japanese paintings are hidden. Michael's father believed that his son was trying to commit the robbery until some friends pointed out that Michael's dead body was holding the gun in the wrong hand. He now accuses Morris of foul play.

Michael's Father:
そ...それじゃあ、マイケル　は　強盗　じゃなく...
So ... sore jā, Maikeru wa gōtō ja naku
well then　　　(name) as for robber wasn't
"So then, Michael wasn't committing a robbery ..." (PL2)

やっぱりすべてお前　が　仕組んだ　の　か...
yappari subete omae ga shikunda no ka ...
after all all you (sub.) contrived/planned (explan.) (?)
"You set up the whole thing after all." (PL2)

Morris: やっぱり? やっぱり とは どう いう こと だ?
Yappari? Yappari to wa dō iu koto da?
after all after all as for what say thing is

まさか、あんた　最初　から　俺　を　疑って...
Masaka, anta saisho kara ore o utagatte ...
surely not you beginning from I/me (obj.) doubt

"'After all?' What do you mean, 'after all?' You can't mean that you suspected me from the beginning!" (PL2)

© Katsushika & Urasawa / *Mastā Kiiton*, Shogakukan

- *gōtō* can mean "robber" or "robbery."
- *masaka* is used to indicate that an idea or belief seems impossible or unbelievable.
- *anta* is a colloquial contraction of *anata* ("you").
- *ore* is a rough/informal masculine word for "me."

I tried it, but . . .

This rookie salesman has not sold a single car in his first two months, and he is starting to doubt if he has what it takes to do sales. (Car salesmen in Japan go around to call on individual as well as corporate customers.)

© Fujiko Fujio / *Yūmu*, Shogakukan

Salesman:　やっぱりむいてない の　　かもしれない なあ...
Yappari muite-nai no kamoshirenai nā...
after all　not suited to　(explan.)　maybe　(emph.)
"Maybe I'm just not suited (to this job) after all." (PL2)

- *muite-nai* is a contraction of *muite-inai,* from *muku* ("face/point toward").
  Muku refers to orientation, and by extension, to suitability.

I knew it

The *seijinshiki* is an annual coming-of-age ceremony for all young people who turn 20 that year. Rokurō was not planning to attend, but the "president" of the small garage where he works gave him a suit and shoes, and he decided to go after all. On the way, he stopped to help fix a stalled ambulance and got his new outfit dirty. Now he is at the ceremony wishing he had skipped the whole thing.

© Saigan Ryōhei / *San chōme no Yūhi*, Shogakukan

Rokurō:　やっぱり 来る んじゃなかった...
Yappari kuru n ja nakatta...
after all　come　shouldn't have
"I knew I shouldn't have come." (PL2)

友達　　も　知り合い　も　　いない　　　　し...
Tomodachi mo shiriai mo inai shi...
friend　　and　acquaintance also not exist/aren't here and
寂しい　　思い　　を　する だけ なん だ から。
Sabishii omoi o suru dake nan da kara.
sad/lonely thought/feeling (obj.)　do　only　(explan.)　is because
**"I don't have any friends or acquaintances here . . .
I just feel lonely."** (PL2)

Expressing a preference

Faced with a decision between two different types of photo albums, this girl states her choice. She is worried that if the pictures aren't permanently attached, her father will take them out and forget to put them back.

© Haruki Etsushi / *Jarinko Chie*, Futabasha

<u>Chie-chan:</u> やっぱり ノリ で はる やつ が ええ な。
Yappari nori de haru yatsu ga ē na.
really   paste/glue with attach one/type (subj.) good (emph.)
"Really, one that you attach (pictures) to with glue is good."
"I guess I'd really better get one that you glue (the pictures) into." (PL2)

- *yatsu* is usually used to refer (not very politely) to a person and translated as "guy," but can also refer to a thing, carrying the meaning of "type."
- *ē* is a dialect version of *ii*, "good/preferable."
- *na* is a masculine expression of emphasis, but women and girls often use it when they are talking to themselves or to children.

Making a choice

The baseball team's manager is having trouble deciding who to put at second base and right field, as all of his remaining players seem to have some flaws. He has just watched one of them make some nice defensive plays in practice, and that helps him make up his mind.

<u>Manager:</u> んー... / やっぱ セカンド に は...
N– / Yappa sekando ni wa ...
Hmm   in the end/after all second   at as-for
"Hmm, so I guess at second ..." (PL2)

© Hara Hidenari/ *Yattarō jan*, Shogakukan

Truisms

General truths and obvious facts can be stated with *yappari*. This is an example of re-confirmation of something believed or expected to be true. The man in this scene is lamenting the fact that the women they were supposed to meet at a bar went off with some wealthier customers.

Man: やっぱり　金　だ　よ　金。
Yappari   kane da yo   kane.
after all/really money is (emph.) money
"Of course it's money, you know, money." (PL2)

男前　　だけじゃあ　もてねえ　　よ。
Otokomae dake   jā   mote-nē   yo.
handsome only with   won't be popular (emph.)
"You won't be popular if all you are is handsome."
(PL2)

- *otokomae* is an old word for "handsome," still used in some dialects. Today one more often hears the katakana word ハンサム (*hansamu*), rendered from the English.
- *motenē* is a corruption of *motenai*, the plain negative of *moteru*, "be popular."

© Jōji Akiyama / *Haguregumo*, Shogakukan

The expression *Shokuyoku no aki* could be rendered as "Autumn, the season when appetites are good." The idea is that in summer, when the weather is hot, most people don't have much of an appetite, but in autumn the weather begins to cool off, stimulating appetites, and there are plenty of appetizing foods available. Of all the delicious foods associated with autumn, *matsutake* mushrooms are perhaps the pinnacle. In this manga, one small basket goes for ¥50,000.

Man: 食欲　　の　秋　　といえば
Shokuyoku no aki   to ieba
appetite   ('s) autumn if you say
やっぱり　松茸　　だ　な。
yappari   matsutake   da na.
after all (mushroom type) is (emph.)

"When you say appetite's autumn, it just has to be *matsutake* mushrooms."
"Yep, it's *matsutake* mushrooms for autumn, all right." (PL2)

© Nakashima Tōru / *Puro no Hitorigoto*, Shogakukan

Lesson 28 • *Abunai*

As an adjective, *abunai* means "dangerous/hazardous," but it's also used like the English "Look out!/Watch out!" — to warn someone of impending danger, or as a reaction to a dangerous situation. *Abunai* is one of several adjectives that are used as exclamations in Japanese. Here are some of the others.

Japanese word	Meaning as an adjective	Meaning as an exclamation
Itai! (いたい)	sore/painful	Ouch!
Atsui! (熱い)	hot	Ouch! (from burn)
Urusai! (うるさい)	noisy/bothersome	Shut up!
Sugoi! (凄い)	incredible/terrible	Wow!

This use of adjectives as exclamations is facilitated by the fact that it is not necessary to specify a subject in Japanese—the adjective can stand alone as a complete thought.

Here are some examples of how the word *abunai* is used; first as an exclamation, then as an adjective.

"Look out!" (1)

Mochi "rice cakes" are a traditional food at New Year's. There are mochi-making machines now, but it's still not uncommon to have a neighborhood *mochi-tsuki taikai* (餅つき大会), or "mochi-making party," where everyone joins in to make mochi the old-fashioned way — by pounding steamed glutinous rice with a heavy wooden mallet. One person swings the mallet while another turns the mochi, so timing is crucial to avoid a smashed hand. Here, a small boy takes a turn with the mallet, but brings it down suddenly without regard for the timing.

Boy: たーっ!
Tā–!
"Hayaa!" (PL2)

Sound FX: ブンッ
Bun!
(effect of mallet coming down suddenly)

Onlooker: あ、あぶないっ!!
A, Abunai!!
"Hey, look out!" (PL2)

© Nakashima Tōru / *Puro no Hitorigoto*, Shogakukan

"Look out!" (2)

Just in time, this man pulls the child out of the path of a speeding truck. This one panel probably covers a brief span of time, and we can assume that the man started to say *Abunai!* as soon as he realized the child was in danger, rather than after the fact.

© Nakagawa Isami / *Kuma no Pūtaro*, Shogakukan

Man: 危ない！
Abunai!
"Look out!" (PL2)

Sound FX: ブォー
Buō–
(sound of the truck zooming by)

Driver: スピー
Supii
(effect of dozing; a bubble coming out of the nose is used to indicate that someone has dozed off)

"Look out!" (3)

Some friends have gathered at Narumi's house for dinner. When she opens the cabinet to get a bowl, everything falls out.

© Saimon Fumi / *Asunaru Hakusho,* Shogakukan

Sound FX: ガララン
Gararan
(clatter of falling dishes)

Narumi: キャ！
Kya!
"Yikes!" (PL2)

Kakei: 危ない!!
Abunai!!
"Look out!" (PL2)

A dialect form

The dog is curious about the sputtering fuse on a Roman candle. This character, Beranmei Tōchan, speaks in the Tokyo *shitamachi* (下町, "low city") dialect in which *ai* sounds frequently come out as *ei*.

© Tachibanaya Kikutarō / *Beranmei Tōchan,* Take Shobō

Tōchan: あっこら　ポチ　あぶねいっ
A! kora Pochi abunei!
ah　hey　(dog's name)　danger
"Ah! Hey! Pochi, look out!" (PL2)

Sound FX: シューッ
Shū–!
(sound of burning fuse)

Kazuo: わーっ
Wā–!
"Ahhhhh!"

• *kora* is a verbal reprimand, used to get the attention of someone who is doing something dangerous or inappropriate.

Close to the edge

Their favorite sumo wrestler is about to be pushed out of the ring. This use of *abunai* refers to being in a tight/difficult situation—about to lose the match—rather than being in any kind of physical danger.

Announcer: 鬼童山、一気に　寄る!
Kidōsan ikki ni yoru
(name) in one shot push
"Kidōsan presses forward in a single burst!" (PL2)

Spectators: わーーっ!!
Wā–!!
"Ahhh"

Spectators: 危なーい!
Abuna–i!
"Look out!" (PL2)

© Ichimaru / *Okamisan*, Shogakukan

In danger

As an adjective, *abunai* can mean "in danger/at risk," as well as "dangerous." Here a media group is wondering how they can expose and topple a corrupt politician and company official without putting their colleague's job in danger.

© Inose & Hirokane / *Rasuto Nyūsu*, Shogakukan

Man: 軽はずみな　　発言　は よせ。
Karuhazumi-na hatsugen wa yose.
hasty/rash statement(s) as-for stop

我々　　が　下手に　動く　と　日野さん の クビ　が 危ない。
Wareware ga heta ni ugoku to Hino-san no kubi ga abunai.
we (subj.) unskillfully move if/when (name)-hon 's neck/job (subj.) in danger
"Quit making rash utterances. If we move unskillfully, Hino's neck will be in danger."
"Don't make such rash statements. If we do something stupid, it could cost Hino his job."
(PL2)

- *kubi* literally means "neck," but the expression *kubi ni naru* means "be fired," so in the context of work or job situations, *kubi* is a reference to being fired.
- the particle *ga* (が) rather than *wa* (は) is more likely to be used in this kind of situation, but you rarely have to worry about misunderstandings, since context will make the distinction clear.

Dangerous

This child is frustrated because his mother won't let him do anything for himself. Here, she takes the knife away from him because it is dangerous.

© Takeuchi Akira / *Garushia-kun*, Futabasha

Mother: ママ が むいてあげよう ね。 包丁 危ない もん ね。
Mama ga muite ageyō ne. Hōchō abunai mon ne.
mom (subj.) peel for you (colloq.) knife dangerous thing (colloq.)
"Mama will peel it for you. Knives are dangerous things, aren't they."
"I'll peel it for you. Knives are dangerous, huh." (PL2)

Boy: かえして よォ。
Kaeshite yo–.
return (emph.)
"Give it baaack." (PL2)

- *hōchō* is a kitchen/cooking knife.
- she has omitted the particle (subject/topic marker) after *hōchō*, but it would have been *wa* (は).
- *kaeshite* is from the verb kaesu ("give back/return").

The crowd at this concert came to see their favorite group, but they are being forced to sit through an unknown singer's warm-up act, and they are starting to get rowdy.

Man: ここ は 危ない!! ...行こう ぜ、マユ!
Koko wa abunai! Ikō ze, Mayu.
here as-for dangerous let's go (emph.) (name)
"It's getting dangerous! Let's get out of here, Mayu!" (PL2)

Mayu: え...!?
E...!?
"Huh?" (PL2)

Crowd: カエレ カエレ カエレ
Kaere kaere kaere
return return return
"Go Home, Go Home, Go Home..." (PL2)

- *ikō* is the plain/abrupt volitional ("let's ~") form of the verb *iku* ("go").
- *ze* is an emphatic particle used in informal/abrupt masculine speech.
- *kaere* is the abrupt command form of the verb *kaeru* ("return/go home").

© Tsuchida Seiki / *Orebushi*, Shogakukan

Dangerous and in danger

Obatarian rides her scooter down the middle of the road, without a helmet and carrying a child on her back. In this case, she is in danger herself, as well as creating a hazard for other drivers.

© Hotta Katsuhiko / *Obatarian*, Take Shobō

Driver: あぶねー なー 道 の まん中 を...
Abunē nā Michi no mannaka o...
dangerous (colloq.) road/street 's middle (obj.)
"That sure is dangerous, (riding a scooter) down the middle of the road." (PL2)

Sound FX: ポトポト...
Poto poto...
("Putt-putt" of the scooter)

- once again we see the form *abunē*. Changing *ai* to *ei* or *ee* can also be masculine slang rather than a specific dialect, as is the case here.

A slang variation — *yabai*

Almost identical in meaning to *abunai*, the word *yabai* is very much slang, and suitable for use only in informal situations. In this example, Kariage-kun is about to lose a game of chess.

© Ueda Masashi / *Kariage-kun*, Futabasha

Opponent: チェック
Chekku
"Check." (PL2)

Kariage-kun: ウーム。そう きた か。
Ūmu. Sō kita ka
hmm like that came is it
"Hmm, so you came like that, did you?"
"Hmm, so that's your move, huh?" (PL2)

Friend: やばい よ お前。
Yabai yo omae.
in danger (emph.) you
"You're in trouble." (PL2)

キング と クイーン とられちゃう よ。
Kingu to kuiin torarechau yo.
king and queen will be taken (regret) (emph.)
"Your king and queen are going to be taken." (PL2)

- *torarechau* is a contraction of *torarete shimau*; *torarete* from the verb *torareru* ("be taken"), and *shimau*, used with the *-te* form of other verbs to indicate that the result will be undesirable/unfortunate.
- actually, the king can't be taken in chess, but this is still a good illustration of the word *yabai*.

35

BASIC JAPANESE through comics

Lesson 29 • *Stylized kanji*

Many *kanji* (漢字, "Chinese characters") are actually highly stylized pictures. For ex ample, the kanji for "river" (川) started out as a drawing of a river that became increasingly stylized until it evolved into its present form. In the graphic arts, however, sometimes the process goes backwards, and kanji are altered to look more like the thing they represent, usually with a humorous twist. (The phonetic symbols *hiragana* and *katakana* can also be given the same kind of graphic twist.) In this issue we give you some examples of these "visual puns."

Enlivening manga titles

Manga are a visual medium, so it's not surprising that the artists will be creative with the lettering and kanji in the titles. The strip *Neko de Gomen!* ("Excuse Me for Being a Cat") is about a girl who changes into a half-human, half-cat form when she gets upset. In the title, the kanji 猫 (*neko*, "cat") has been altered to look like a cat's face, and the *daku-ten* (the diacritical marks that change *te* [て] to *de* [で] and *ko* [こ] to *go* [ご]) are drawn as paw prints. Finally, the tip of the ん is a cat's tail.

© Nagano Akane / *Neko de Gomen!*, Kōdansha

猫 で ごめん!
Neko de Gomen!
cat am-thus sorry/forgive me
Excuse Me for Being a Cat!

The title for the gag manga *Kyōryū Kānibaru* ("Dinosaur Carnival") is stylized to look like a dinosaur's spiked tail and jagged teeth. The series features talking dinosaurs with human characteristics.

© Ueda Etsu / *Kyōryū Kānibaru*, Shogakukan

恐竜 カーニバル
Kyōryū Kānibaru
Dinosaur Carnival

One of the most common tricks is putting a star in the upper part of the kanji 星 (*hoshi*, "star/planet"). 日 represents "sun," so the ancient Chinese who made up the character 星 apparently incorporated 日 because stars, planets and the sun are all radiant heavenly bodies. In any case, the best-known example of a ☆ in the 日 of 星 is probably Takahashi Rumiko's popular *Urusei Yatsura* series, but there are plenty of others.

© Takahashi Rumiko / *Urusei Yatsura,* Shogakukan

うる星 やつら
Urusei   Yatsura
Annoying People or **People from Planet Uru**

- the title *Urusei Yatsura* is a pun based on the word *urusai* ("pesky/obnoxious/annoying"). In certain styles of slang masculine speech, the vowel combination -*ai*- changes to -*ei*-, so *urusai* becomes *urusei*. The kanji for "star/planet," 星, can be read *sei* in combinations, and is used here for the *sei* in *urusei*. Written this way, *Urusei* can also mean "the planet Uru." The word *yatsura* is simply a plural form of *yatsu,* a slang word for "guy/fellow." The *Urusei Yatsura* series has been translated into English, and known in in the US as "Those Annoying Aliens."

© Unose Ken'ichi / *Rotte no Hoshi,* Shogakukan

ロッテの 星
Rotte   no hoshi
Lotte   's (name)
Lotte's Hoshi/Star

- Lotte refers to the Lotte Orions, which was once a Japanese professional baseball team. (The team name has since been changed to the Lotte Marines, Lotte being the huge candy company that sponsors the team.) In the manga series, Lotte's pitcher is named Hoshi, a convenient coincidence, since he is also their "star."

The presence of ghosts or spirits is often indicated by 火の玉 (*hi no tama,* lit., "fireball," similar to a will-o'-the-wisp) in Japanese folklore. The manga series *Yūyū Hakusho* ("Astral Visit Report"), about a young "spiritual detective" who fights evil supernatural beings, uses *hi no tama* as part of the kanji 幽 (*yū,* used to refer to spirits or the spirit world).

幽遊   白書
Yūyū   Hakusho
astral visit white paper/report
Astral Visit Report

- the kanji 遊 refers to "play," but also carries the meaning of "meander(ing)/wander(ing)."

© Togashi Yoshihiro / *Yūyū Hakusho,* Shueisha

More manga titles

This story is about a man who discovers a warp in time and tries to use it for betting on the horses, but is eventually trapped by it. The leftmost part of 時 (日, representing the sun) has been drawn as a clock.

© Okazaki Jirō / *After Zero, Short Short*, Shogakukan

時　の向こう側
Toki　no　Mukō-gawa
time　's　　other side
The Other Side of Time

A racy story from the weekly manga magazine *Shūkan Manga Times* has the title *Juku-jo, Mijuku-jo, Sōjuku-jo*. The kanji for "woman/female" (女, *onna*), has been drawn as a pair of women's legs. Other small touches include hearts in the kanji 熟 and lips in 早.

© Toyoda & Tanemura / *Juku-jo, Mijuku-jo, Sōjuku-jo*, Hōbunsha

熟女　　　　　未熟女　　　　　早熟女
Juku-jo　　　　*Mijuku-jo*　　　　*Sōjuku-jo*
mature/ripe girl　not yet mature girl　fast/early mature girl.
Mature Girl, Immature Girl, Early-maturing Girl

Set in the days of feudal Japan, *Sansū Ōji* is a parody of samurai drama manga. The "math prince" is a right triangle-wielding mercenary mathematician who helps those in mathematical distress—for a fee. In addition to freeing people from arithmetical oppression, he also takes on evil mathematicians.

算数 王子
Sansū　Ōji
Math Prince

© Nakayama Yūya / *Math Prince*, Shogakukan

Ads and product names

The Yupiteru cordless answering-machine phone is called *Koko Ose Irumi.* Buttons on the phone light up to guide users through its various operations. The kanji 押, meaning "push," has been rendered as a hand with an extended, pushing finger.

ココ 押せ イルミ
Koko   Ose   Irumi
here   push   illumi(nation)
Push-Here Illumination

- *irumi* can be short for "illumination," or "illuminated."
- *ose* is an abrupt command form, but that's OK in this kind of application.

A visual and verbal pun

Clothing manufacturer Renown named its anti-bacterial odor-resistant socks 通勤快足(*tsūkin kaisoku,* "commuting [with] pleasant feet"), a pun based on 通勤快速 (*tsūkin kaisoku,* "commuting express [train]"). The pun is made possible by the fact that the kanji for "speed" (速) and the kanji for "foot/leg" (足) can both be read *soku.* It's made even more viable by the fact that the other kanji, 快 (*kai*), really means "pleasant." 快速 (*kaisoku*), the word for "express [train]" literally means "pleasant speed," i.e. making few stops, so the combination 快足 (*kaisoku*), although not a real word, is a good way to express the idea of "pleasant/happy" feet.

The kanji 足 (*ashi*, "foot/leg") has been drawn with a footprint on top, somewhat ironic if you consider that the actual kanji is a stylized depiction of the side view of a leg, with the foot on the bottom.

通勤　　快足
Tsūkin　Kaisoku
commuting pleasant feet
Commuting (with) Pleasant Feet

– is a pun based on –

通勤快速
Tsūkin Kaisoku
Commuting Express (Train)

レナウン 抗菌　　防臭 ソックス
Renaun　kōkin　bōshū　sokkusu
(name)   anti-bacterial odor-resistant socks
Renown Anti-Bacterial Odor-Resistant Socks

Game software

The name of the game is Soft-Boiled Hero—the name of a video game for the *Sūpā Famikon* ("Super Nintendo" in the US), that is. The unlikely hero is a soft-boiled egg called Eggman (エッグマン, *Egguman*). Eggman battles his way through 12 scenarios, meeting such foes as the Egg Monster and the Hard-Boiled Army. The kanji 半熟 (*hanjuku*) literally means "half-ripe" or "half-mature," but refers to "soft-boiled" when it comes to eggs. The first stroke of 半 has been replaced with Eggman's likeness. The kana below the title show that the kanji normally read as *eiyū* ("hero") are to be read *hiirō,* from the English.

Top: ああ, 世界　よ　　半熟　なれ...!!
Ā,　　sekai　yo　hanjuku　nare...!!
ah　　world　(address) soft-boiled become
Ah, world, become soft boiled!

Center: 半熟　英雄
Hanjuku　Eiyū
Soft-Boiled Hero

Bottom: はんじゅくヒーロー
Hanjuku　　　　　Hiirō
Soft-Boiled Hero

- the line *Ā sekai yo, hanjuku nare* is a parody of the well-known line *Ā seijōki yo, eikyū nare* (ああ星条旗よ永久なれ), reputedly a line from the Japanese version of the American national anthem, but translating literally as "Oh, may the stars and stripes last forever."

Toys

***Gaijin tarento* and physical fitness instructor** Chuck Wilson teamed up with toy-maker Tomy to produce these sets of finger-strengthening toys called ゆびトレマシーン (*yubi tore mashiin*, "finger training machine"). There are three varieties, and they come boxed with a small bag of candy. (A cardboard cut-out "doll" of Wilson is also included.) The kanji for *yubi* ("finger") is 指, but it's written in hiragana here, with fingers forming the *yu* and the *bi*.

Top: チャック•ウイルソン　の
Chakku　•　Uiruson　　no
Chuck Wilson's

Bottom: ゆびトレマシーン
yubi　tore　mashiin
Finger Training Machine

- *tore* is an abbreviation of *torēningu,* from English "training," and *mashiin* is from English "machine."

Magazine headlines

The kanji for "forest" (森, *mori*) is simply the kanji for tree (木, *ki*) repeated three times. 森の めぐみ (*Mori no Megumi,* "Blessings of the Forests") was the title of an article in *Sunday Mainichi* about deforestation in Japan. One of the trees in the kanji 森 has been drawn as real tree, instead of the usual stylized pictograph.

© 1992 Sunday Mainichi

森　のめぐみ
Mori　no　Megumi
Forest　's　blessing
The Blessing(s) of Forests

* *megumi* is the noun form of the verb
  megumu ("bless/bestow").

The recession hit everyone, even kids. The video game magazine *Famikon Tsūshin* ran a feature entitled ビンボーゲームライフ(*Binbō Gēmu Raifu,* "Game Life for the Poor"), about enjoying games during tough economic times. The feature outlined such strategies as playing demo games for free at department stores and entering drawings to win game cartridges. *Binbō* can be written with the kanji 貧乏, but here it is written in katakana, using bottles (*bin* in Japanese) to form the *bin* and sticks (*bō* in Japanese) to make the *bō.*

© 1993 Famikon Tsūshin

<u>**Top:**</u> 不況 に 打ち勝つ
Fukyō　ni　uchikatsu
recession to conquer/overcome
Beat the Recession

<u>**Center:**</u> ビンボー ゲーム ライフ
Binbō　Gēmu　Raifu
poor　game　life
Game Life for the Poor

<u>**Bottom:**</u> 緊急　　特集
Kinkyū　tokushū
emergency special edition
Urgent Special Report

BASIC JAPANESE through comics

Lesson 30 • *Maitta*

Whenever you hear someone say *maitta* as an interjection, you know they are somehow in trouble or distressed. *Maitta* can be used to admit defeat, like "Uncle" or "I give up" in English — including cases of a good humored defeat. It can be a mild exclamation of chagrin like "Geez/Darn it all/What a bummer!" Or it can be similar to *komatta* (see Basic Japanese No. 15) in indicating that you are in a fix, worried, at a loss for what to do or say.

Maitta comes from *mairu* (参る), which refers to the act of approaching or moving close to a superior and is used as a humble verb for "(I) go" or "(I) come." One of the idiomatic uses stemming from this is "(go) worship/pray at a shrine." So the word has always been associated with submission/supplication. Considering these implications of *maitta*, it's not hard to see certain connections with the meanings in the examples we present here, but we haven't been able to find any theories about just how these usages might have evolved.

When *maitta* is used as an interjection, an emphatic particle almost always follows it (*na*, *wa*, *ne*, *yo*, etc.). As some of our examples show, it can also be used as the verb of a regular sentence to convey essentially the same meaning.

"What a bummer"

This hostess bar is having a rough time because of the poor economy.

© Kunitomo Yasuyuki / *Paro paro*, Shogakukan

Proprietress: まいった わ ねー。 全然 客 来ない わ よォ。
Maitta wa nē. Zenzen kyaku konai wa yo—.
in a fix/bind (fem.) (colloq.) at all customer(s) don't come (fem.) (emph.)
"What a bummer. No customers at all." (PL2)

"Sound" FX: がらあんん
Garānn
(effect of being empty/deserted)

Hostess: ああ、 バブル の 時代 が なつかしい。
Ā, baburu no jidai ga natsukashii.
ah bubble 's time/era (subj.) is fondly remembered
"Ah, I miss the bubble (economy) era." (PL2)

• the Japanese word for "bubble" is *awa* (泡), but a katakana rendering of the English is used when referring to the overheated "bubble" economy of the late 80s and early 90s.

"What to do?"

This section chief (*kachō*) usually gets someone else to make copies for him, but this time he is at the office by himself.

Kachō: あれ、／ この ボタン でない　とすると...
Are,　／　Kono botan　de nai　to suru to ...
huh　this　button　is not　when you consider that
"Huh? Well if it isn't this button, then . . ." (PL2)

Sound FX: カチャ カチャ
kacha　kacha
(clicking sound of pushing a button)

Kachō: まいった なあ。
Maitta　nā.
in a fix　(colloq.)
"What do I do now?"

"Dang"

The hero of this story about *shōgi*, or Japanese chess, fell asleep in his room and is now late for an important game.

Shōsuke: まいった な... どこ の 部屋 だったっけ か?
Maitta　na... Doko no heya datta kke ka?
be at a loss (colloq.) where 's room was it ?
"Dang, which room was it now?"

みんな 同じ よう で、わかんねぇ な。
Minna onaji yō de, wakannē na.
all same appearance are-and can't tell (colloq.)
"They all look alike; I can't tell."

- *datta kke* (or often *da kke*) is used after a question word (*doko*, "where" in this case) when you can't bring to mind something you used to know or are trying to remember.
- *wakannē* is a contraction/corruption of *wakaranai*, the negative plain past of *wakaru*, "know/understand."

© Nōjō Jun'ichi / *Gekka no Kishi*, Shogakukan

Physical distress

Maitta can also be used when you're hot or tired. In this scene, Muraki has just returned from running some company errands on a blisteringly hot day.

© Hayashi & Takai / *Yamaguchi Roppeita,* Shogakukan

> **Muraki:** いやー まいった す、暑くて 暑くて。
> *Iyā   maitta   su, atsukute atsukute*
> well   worn out is/am   hot   hot
> **"Wow, I've had it, it's so hot."**   (PL2-3)

- *iya* (sometimes lengthened to *iyā*) is actually a statement of disgust or chagrin, but here is used more as a verbal warm-up.
- *maitta su* is a contraction of *maitta desu,* a kind of colloquial/informal alternate to the PL3 *mairimashita.* Muraki almost always shortens *desu* to *su.*

A star jockey has been getting threatening letters, and then receives a package containing a small voodoo doll of him with a pin through the chest. Understandably worried, he is negotiating with some professional bodyguards.

© Kurotsuchi & Mitsuyama / *Yōjinbō Urimasu,* Shogakukan

> **Ukon:** だから 僕、
> *Dakara boku,*
> because/so I/me
> 夜 も ロクに 眠れない ん です。
> *yoru mo roku ni nemurenai   n   desu.*
> night also sufficiently/well can't sleep (explan.) is
> 実際 参っています。
> *Jissai maitte-imasu.*
> really   am in a bind.
> **"So I can't even sleep well at night. It's really getting to me."** (PL2)

- *roku* means "good" or "well," but is usually used with a negative to mean "not well"→"bad/poor," etc.

At a loss for words

Former college rugby star Naoto heads out for a late night snack after putting his son to bed. The proprietress recognizes him from an old magazine article.

© Hirokane Kenshi / *Papa to Ikiru*, Shogakukan

Azakami: あなた の こと ね、提さん。
Anata   no koto   ne, Tsutsumi-san.
you   's thing isn't it (name-hon.)
"This is you, isn't it, Tsutsumi-san."

Magazine: 堤　　直人
Tsutsumi Naoto

- *anata no koto* looks like "the fact/thing of you," but means "(about) you."
- the kanji 提 in Azakami's dialog balloon is apparently a misprint, and should be 堤, as it appears in the magazine she is holding.

Naoto: まいった　　　　　な、その通り です。
Maitta   na, sono tōri desu.
don't know what to say (colloq.) just like that   is
"This is embarrassing. It's just as you say."
(PL3)

Etsuko was ready to marry this man five years ago, but broke up with him because she saw him in a love hotel district with another woman. She now finds out that the woman was his sister, who worked in the area of the hotels. She had thought that he was just toying with her affections, but he was actually hoping to marry her. Now she decides to pretend that she was never serious about him.

© Kunitomo Yasuyuki / *Paro paro*, Shogakukan

Etsuko:

アハハハ。
A ha ha ha.
(laugh)
"Ah, ha ha ha."

そっかァ、参っちゃったな。
Sokkā,   maitchatta na.
is that so   don't know what to say

あなた が そこまで 私 に 本気 だった なんて。
Anata ga soko made watashi ni honki datta   nante.
you   (subj.) that much/far I/me about serious was   the very idea
"Is that so? What can I say? I never knew you were so serious about me." (PL2)

- the *sokkā* and the *na* after *maitchatta* give her speech a somewhat rough tone which serves to mask her disappointment.

"I lose/give up"

Yoshii is negotiating the price of a catered party with Akiba. It was supposed to cost ¥25,000 per person, but now Akiba says ¥30,000, with all drinks included. Yoshii reluctantly agrees when Akiba makes a rather high-pressure pitch.

© Saimon Fumi / *Asunaro Hakusho*, Shogakukan

Akiba: ありがとうございます、では　一人　三万円　で。
Arigatō gozaimasu,　　　　　dewa　hitori　sanman-en　de.
thank you　　　　　　　　　with that　one person　30,000 yen　at
"Thank you. Then 30,000 yen apiece it is." (PL3-4)

Yoshii: まいった　な。　かなわない　よ。
Maitta　　na.　Kanawanai　yo.
give up　(colloq.)　am no match　(emph.)
"OK, I give up. I'm no match for you." (PL2)

Imano works at the front desk of a hotel, and has recently heard from his co-workers that it is important to scrutinize people as they leave the hotel to figure out whether they were pleased with the service or not, and then take measures to set things right with the guests who weren't happy. The old pros can tell how the hotel guests feel just by looking at their posture from behind, but Imano can't seem to get the hang of it.

© Ishinomori Shōtarō / *HOTEL*, Shogakukan

Imano: まいった　な。
Maitta　　na.
in a bind　(colloq.)
"I give up." (PL2)

後ろ　　姿　　なんて　　いくら見ても　わかんない　や。
Ushiro　sugata　nante　　ikura mite mo　wakannai　ya.
back/behind　figure/shape　something like　no matter how much I look　don't get it　(emph.)
"No matter how hard I look at them from behind, I just can't tell anything." (PL2)

• *wakannai* is a contraction of *wakaranai*, the negative plain past of *wakaru* ("understand").

A taunt

Commodore Bell has come to Japan on a trading mission, and he's been bragging about his extensive knowledge of Japanese culture. The local magistrate (*bugyō*) takes him out drinking, ordering sake that is neither hot nor cold, but *hitohada,* or "skin temperature."

Bell: 熱く　も　なく　冷たい　の　でも　なく　人肌?
Atsuku　mo　naku　tsumetai　no　demo　naku　hitohada?
hot　also　not　cold　(explan.)　also　not　human skin
"Neither hot nor cold, but skin-temperature?" (PL2)

Bugyō: ゲージン　は　な、熱いか　冷めてえか　だけ　だろ。
Gējin　wa　na,　atsui ka　tsumetē ka　dake　daro.
foreigner(s)　as-for　(colloq.)　hot-or　cold-or　only　right

こっち　は　な、
Kotchi　wa　na,
this direction/us　as-for　(colloq.)

人肌　って　の　も　ある　ん　だ　よ。
hitohada　tte　no　mo　aru　n　da　yo.
human skin　called　(=)　also　have/exist　(explan.)　is　(emph.)
"Foreigners have only hot or cold, don't they. We have what's called 'skin temperature,' too." (PL2)

まいった　か　この　バカ。
Maitta　ka kono　baka.
give up　?　this　idiot
"Do you give up, you idiot?" (PL1-2)

- the bugyō uses a kind of rough speech/dialect in which the word *tsumetai* becomes *tsumetē,* and *gaijin* becomes *gējin.*

© Akiyama Jōji / *Haguregumo,* Shogakukan

"You've got me there"

One of his drinking buddies comments that Haguregumo is a man who has a good feel about him. The barmaid pipes in about what she thinks gives a man that certain aura.

Barmaid: うち　に　したら　です　よ、
Uchi　ni shitara desu　yo,
me　to/as-for　is　(emph.)
"Well, as for me, you know,"

気持ち　の　いい　男　って　の　は、勘定　を
kimochi　no　ii　otoko　tte　no wa, kanjō　o
feeling　(subj.)　good　man　(quote)　(=)　as for　account　(obj.)

きちっと　払って　くれる　人　の　こと　でして　ね。
kichitto　haratte kureru hito no koto deshite　ne.
properly　pay (favor)　person　('s)　case　is　(colloq.)
"a man with a good feel about him is one who keeps his tab paid up." (PL3)

Haguregumo: ありゃ、こりゃ　まいった。
Arya,　korya　maitta.
well　as for this　you've got me
"Oops, guess you've got me there."

- *arya* is a variation of *are,* an expression of surprise or bewilderment.
- *korya* is a contraction of *kore wa* ("as for this").

© Akiyama Jōji / *Haguregumo,* Shogakukan

Lesson 31 • *Sasuga*

When translating a foreign language, there are some words that have a neat and tidy English equivalent, and some that don't. *Sasuga* is one of the latter. The concept of *sasuga*, however, is quite simple and a few good manga examples and a little explanation should be sufficient to clarify it, even for beginners.

Sasuga is translated most simply as "as you'd expect." It's generally an expression of awe or admiration, used when someone who is expected to be good at something proves to be truly skillful or gifted. For example, when Michael Jordan makes a game-winning 3-point shot at the buzzer, you could say, *"sasuga,"* meaning, "That's just what you would have expected from Michael Jordan." *Sasuga* does have some similarity with *yappari* (Basic Japanese No. 27), since it indicates that an outcome is "as expected," but *sasuga* is usually more specifically linked to someone or something's reputation, rather than the expectations of the observer. It's also used mostly in a positive sense, although two of our examples illustrate exceptions. Get this concept down and your Japanese friends will be saying, *"Sasuga nihongo ga umai!"* ("As would be expected of you, your Japanese is good!")

"That's a pro for you."

Watching a pro at work can lead to exclamations of *sasuga*. Here, a customer at a *ryōtei* (traditional Japanese restaurant) is awed by the chef's sashimi-slicing technique.

Customer: さすが、うまい もん です ね。
Sasuga,   umai   mon desu ne.
as expected skillful (emph.) is (colloq.)
"As you'd expect, he's really good."
"That's a pro for you, he's really good!"
(PL3)

Shachō: あたりまえ　や。
Atarimae   ya.
a matter of course   is
"Of course!" (PL2)

• *mon* is a contraction of *mono,* which in this usage serves mainly as emphasis.
• *ya* is a dialect version of *da.*

© Abe & Kurata / *Aji Ichimonme*, Shogakukan

Sasuga + position or title

The experienced caddy Chitta rates a *sasuga* when he tells his client that the opponent's shots are all going left, and points out that this is a good chance to take the lead. Using *sasuga* implies that he fulfills the expectations that people have because of his position/reputation.

© Sakata & Kazama / *Kaze no Daichi*, Shogakukan

Okita: さっすが　　名キャディ！　コース　だけでなく
Sassuga　　mei-kyadii!　Kōsu　dake de naku
as you'd expect　famous/great caddy　course　not only

相手　の　ゴルフ　も　読んでる　んだ。
aite　no gorufu mo　yonderu　n da.
opponent 's　golf　also　is/are reading　(explan.)
"Just as you'd expect from a great caddy. You're not just reading the course, but the opponent's game as well!" (PL2)

Sound FX: ポン
Pon
(sound of a pat on the shoulder)

Chitta: にゃはは、それほど　でも...
Nya ha ha,　Sore hodo　demo...
(laugh)　to that extent　even
"Ah ha ha. It's not such a big deal." (PL2-3)

- saying *sassuga* (doubling the "s" sound) adds emphasis.
- adding the prefix 名 (*mei*, lit. "name") to a title or position is like saying, "the noted/distinguished/celebrated . . ."
- *yonde-ru* is a contraction of *yonde-iru*, from *yomu*, "read."

Determined to earn money to help her grandfather build a house, Izumi takes on a part-time job with some other students helping one of her professors. Her previous training as an OL (office lady) stands her in good stead and her efficiency elicits a *sasuga* from her co-workers.

Sound FX: ガー　ガー
Gā　gā
(sound of a copy machine)

"Sound" FX: さささ
Sa sa sa sa
(effect of repeated quick motions)

Sound FX: とんとん
Ton ton
(sound of tapping papers on table)

"Sound" FX: てきぱき　てきぱき
Tekipaki　tekipaki
(effect of doing something quickly and efficiently)

Sound FX: カタ　カタ　カタ　カタ　カタ
Kata kata kata kata kata
(sound of clacking computer keys)

© Hoshisato Mochiru / *Ribingu Gēmu*, Shogakukan

Co-worker: さすが　　もと　　OL　　だけあって...
Sasuga　moto　o-eru　dake atte...
as might expect　former(ly)　office lady　as might be expected from
"True to form for a former OL . . ." (PL2)

- *dake atte* ("as might be expected from ～") is similar in meaning to *sasuga* and is frequently used in combination with it.

For someone you look up to

Ton-chan has been implanted with a seed that bestows super-human strength as long as the sun is shining on him. In a fight, he rips a tree out of the ground by its roots, but then clouds block the sun, he loses his power, and the tree falls on him. When the sun comes out again seconds later, he regains his strength and pushes the tree off with one hand. His little sister expresses her admiration with *sasuga*—implying she never doubted he could do it.

© Takahashi Rumiko / *Urusei Yatsura,* Shogakukan

"Sound" FX: ばっ
Ba!
(effect of a sudden movement)

Asuka: さすが　は　おにいさま。
Sasuga wa onii-sama.
as expected　as for　older brother
"That's my big brother, all right."　(PL3-4)

- the *wa* after *sasuga* is optional in this kind of usage.

Seizō has tracked down his older brother Keikichi, who left his son's home eight years ago to live alone. Keikichi had felt restricted living with his son, and decided to move out and continue his career as a roofer even though he was almost sixty years old. Seizō has just tried to convince him to go back with his son, but finally realized that Keikichi was happy and doing well on his own. Now Seizō has a new respect for his older brother.

Seizō: いくつ　になっても さすが、　兄貴　だ。
Ikutsu ni natte mo sasuga, aniki da.
how many (years)　becomes even　after all　big brother is
"No matter how old we get, he is, after all, my big brother." (PL2)

- *ikutsu* is literally "how much," but when used with a person refers to age.
- in this example, *sasuga* is similar to *yahari* ("as expected," see Basic Japanese No. 27), but implies a feeling of respect.
- *aniki* is a slang/informal word for "older brother."

© Utsumi & Taniguchi / *Hitobito Shiriizu,* Shogakukan

Outcome is what one would expect

When referring to an outcome, *sasuga* usually has positive implications, but this example is an exception. In this case, *sasuga* gives something of a sarcastic tone.

Employee: 会社　　に　2晩　泊まる　と
Kaisha ni futa-ban tomaru to
company/office at 2 nights stay over if/when
<u>**"Staying at the office two nights in a row . . ."**</u>

さすがに　　汗くさい　なー。
sasuga ni ase-kusai nā.
of course/really stinking of sweat (colloq.)
". . . just as you'd expect, I really stink."
(PL2)

Sound FX: くん
Kun
(sound of smelling/sniffing)

- *sasuga ni* could be replaced with *yahari/yappari* ("as expected/naturally") in this example, but *sasuga ni* feels a bit more emphatic — "I *really* stink."

© Akizuki Risu / *OL Shinkaron*, Kodansha

Dr. Bellmeyer is an expert at analyzing photos taken by spy satellites. His crew has just used satellite photos to locate a missile site in the Middle East, and he is amazed at the satellite's capabilities.

© Saitō Takao / *Gorugo 13*, Shogakukan

Dr. Bellmeyer:
さすがに、　KH-13　軍事　　偵察　　衛星!
Sasuga ni, kei-etchi jūsan gunji teisatsu eisei!
as you'd expect (name) military reconnaissance satellite

信じがたい　解像度　だ!
Shinjigatai kaizōdo da!
hard to believe resolution is
"That's a KH-13 military reconnaissance satellite for you! Unbelievable resolution!" (PL2)

- adding the suffix *-gatai* to a verb gives the meaning "hard to . . ." The verb here is *shinjiru*, "believe," so *shinjigatai* = "hard to believe."
- the scientist's name is written ベルマイヤ (*Berumaiya*) in katakana, so the English spelling Bellmeyer seems like a reasonable guess.

Living up to a reputation

Mr. Nakamura appears to be a harmless, aging Japanese tourist, but he is actually an assassin. His camera is booby-trapped to jab the user in the eye with a poisoned needle when the shutter button is pressed. He asks his unsuspecting victim, the vice-president of an electronics company, to take his picture. The victim is impressed that there seems to be a zoom feature built into the small, automatic camera.

Victim:
さすが　　　メイド・イン・ジャパンです　な。
Sasuga　　　meido　　in　　Japan　desu　　na.
as you'd expect made　　in　　Japan　is　(colloq.)
<u>**"This certainly lives up to the reputation of 'made in Japan'."**</u> (PL3)

Mr. Nakamura:
セントポール　寺院　が　入る　ように　お願いします。
Sento Pōru　　　jiin　ga hairu　yō ni　o-negai shimasu.
Saint Paul　　　cathedral (subj.) enter　so that　　　　please
"Please get Saint Paul's Cathedral in the background." (PL3)

© Katsushika & Urasawa / *Mastā Kiiton*, Shogakukan

Two rival companies are in the beginning stages of preparing bids for an important construction project. They each want to find out what the other is up to, so one of the company presidents gives the other a ring.

© Yamasaki & Kitami / *Tsuri-Baka Nisshi*, Shogakukan

Suzuki: (on other end of phone)
電々　の　件　で　動いてる　そうだ　が、本気　か?
Denden no ken de ugoite-ru sō da ga, honki ka?
(name)　's affair on are moving (hearsay) but serious　?
"I hear you're moving on the NTT project. Are you serious?" (PL2)

- the man pictured in this panel is Amakasu.
- *ugoite-ru* is a contraction of *ugoite-iru*, from *ugoku*, "move."
- 電々 *(denden)* is short for *Denden Kōsha*, which is short for *Nippon Denshin Denwa Kōsha* (Nippon Telegraph and Telephone Public Corporation).

Amakasu: (on other end of phone)
ほう、さすが　　地獄耳!!
Hō,　　　sasuga　jigoku-mimi!
well, as you'd expect　hell-ears
"Well, no wonder they call you *jigoku-mimi!*" (PL2)

- the man pictured in this panel is Suzuki.
- *jigoku-mimi*, lit. "hell-ears," is used to refer to very sharp ears, and by extension, to someone who always seems to be in touch with events, and from whom no secrets can be kept.

Sasuga no

Bumbling salaryman Tanaka-kun asks his boss if there is something he can do, but the boss is reluctant to give him anything difficult or important. This is another example of *sasuga* in a negative context.

© Tanaka Hiroshi / *Tanaka-kun*, Take Shobō

Boss: この 手紙 を ポストに いれてきてくれ!
Kono tegami o posuto ni irete kite kure!
this letter (obj.) post box to put in for me and come back

これ なら さすがの 田中くん も
Kore nara sasuga no Tanaka-kun mo
this if it is reputable/notorious (name-hon.) even/also

ミス は しない だろう。
misu wa shinai darō.
mistake as for won't do probably/surely
"Go mail this letter for me. Even you with your reputation surely can't bungle that." (PL2)

FX: ガックリ
Gakkuri
(effect of being disappointed)

- *irete kite kure* is from the *-te* forms of *ireru* ("insert") and *kuru* ("come"), plus *kure*, which after a *-te* form makes an abrupt request or relatively gentle command. The *-te* form of a verb followed by a form of *kuru* means "(go) do the action and then return to the present location."
- *misu* is an abbreviation of the English word "mistake." *Misu o suru* means "Make a mistake," and *Misu o/wa shinai* is the negative form.
- Tanaka-kun still manages to botch this task, putting the letter in the wrong post box.

A tasty conclusion

These people were all helping Tagawa move out of his office, and it came time for a lunch break. Just as they were trying to decide what to eat, they received a surprise delivery of food from one of Tagawa's friends, a restaurant proprietress.

© Yamasaki & Kitami / *Fukuchan*, Shogakukan

Tagawa: うまい!!
Umai!
"(These are) delicious!"

Friend: 本当 おいしい。
Hontō oishii
really delicious
"You're right, they're good!"

Tagawa: さすが 一流の 料亭 のおにぎりだ。
Sasuga ichi-ryū no ryōtei no onigiri da.
as you'd expect first class restaurant 's rice balls are
"Now that's a first class restaurant's *onigiri*."

- *ryōtei* are traditional Japanese restaurants.
- *onigiri* are balls of rice, often with *umeboshi* (dried, pickled plums) or salmon in the middle. They are standard fare for any kind of "take along" lunch in Japan, much as sandwiches are in the US.

MANGAJIN 's
BASIC JAPANESE through comics

Lesson 32 • Titles

Titles are used in English as well as in Japanese—doctors may be called "Doctor," professors may be addressed as "Professor," the boss may be called "Chief," and, of course, titles are used extensively in the military—but in Japan, titles take on an even greater importance and consequently are much more widely used. The "politeness levels" in the Japanese language and the corresponding social hierarchy make it important to know exactly where you stand, and the extensive use of titles helps keep this structure clear. Titles may be used in place of "you" when speaking to people, or as pronouns when talking about them. A title can even replace the honorific -*san* after someone's name.

Sensei

© Aoyagi Yūsuke / *Senka*, Shogakukan

Thanks in part to pop culture icons such as the Teenage Mutant Ninja Turtles and *The Karate Kid*, even those who know almost nothing about Japanese might realize that *sensei* means "teacher," but the scope of *sensei* is much wider than that of "teacher." The following examples illustrate some of the possibilities.

Yasushi: 先生、 早く 書いて。
    Sensei, hayaku kaite.
    teacher quickly write (please)
    "Please write it quickly, teacher."

- we translated *sensei* directly as "teacher" in this example because English-speaking children in this age group do sometimes call their teachers "teacher," but if Yasushi had been a bit older, we probably would have used, "Mrs./Ms. ～."

© Nitta Tatsuo / *Torishimariyaku Hira Namijirō*, Shogakukan

Sensei can also be used to address anyone who is knowledgeable, skillful, or accomplished in his or her field. The man on the left in this scene is a well-known car critic, and this has earned him the title of *sensei*. He and a reporter are watching the woman he loves, who has just emerged from an apartment building with another man.

Reporter: 先生、 私 は 相手 の 男 が
    Sensei, watashi wa aite no otoko ga
    sir I/me as for companion (=) man (subj.)

    何者 か 知ってます よ。
    nanimono ka shitte-masu yo.
    who (?) know (emph.)
    "Sir, I know who the man with her is." (PL3)

- *shitte-masu* is a slight contraction of *shitte-imasu,* the PL3 of *shitte-iru,* from *shiru,* "know."
- *nanimono* usually has a somewhat derogatory feeling.

Sensei in place of *-san*

As with most titles, *sensei* can replace the honorific *-san* after a person's name.

© Nōjō Jun'ichi / *Gekka no Kishi,* Shogakukan

Office worker: 虎丸　　先生、　お電話 です!!
Toramaru sensei,　o-denwa desu!!
(name)　　(title)　(hon-) phone is

大阪 の　　将棋　　連盟 から!!
Ōsaka no　shōgi　renmei kara!!
(place)　's Japanese chess league/union from
"Mr. Toramaru, it's for you!! From the *shōgi* association in Osaka!!"
(PL3)

- Mr. Toramaru is a teacher/administrator in a *shōgi* (Japanese chess) association. As such he is naturally called *sensei.*

Speaking to a cabinet minister, this man uses the word *sensei* like the pronoun "you."

© Nabeshima & Maekawa / *Hyōden no Torakutā,* Shogakukan

Tsurutake: 光栄 です。　私 も　　飛田　　政権　　実現 のため
Kōei desu. Watashi mo　Tobita　seiken　jitsugen no tame
honor is　I/me also (person's name) political power realization for

粉骨砕身、　　　先生 に従ってまいります。
funkotsu saishin,　sensei　ni shitagatte mairimasu.
(do) my utmost　(title)　will follow (humble)
"I'm honored. I, too, will follow your lead and do everything possible to bring about a Tobita administration." (PL4)

- *funkotsu saishin suru* is "do one's utmost/everything one can." (Some form of *suru* is actually necessary to make the verb form, but Tsurutake has omitted it.) The kanji literally mean "powder (one's) bones and crush (one's) body."
- *mairimasu* is the PL3 form of *mairu,* a humble equivalent of *iku* ("go") or *kuru* ("come").

Hakase

The title *hakase* generally refers to someone with a doctoral degree (but not usually to a medical doctor), and therefore may be translated as "Doctor" or "Professor." This man is the inventor Dr. Slump, and Arale is his android creation.

Arale: はかせ　　　だいスキ!
Hakase　　　daisuki!
Dr./professor like very much/love
"I'm crazy about you, Doctor!" (PL3)

Sound FX: プチュッ
Puchu!
(sound of a kiss)

- *daisuki* means "like very much," but is often used the same way "love" is used in English.

© Toriyama Akira / *Dr. Slump,* Shueisha

The President

The English title "president" corresponds to several more specific titles in Japanese. The president of a country is called *daitōryō* in Japanese (top example), but the president of a company is called *shachō* (bottom example). The president of an association or society would be called *kaichō,* while the president of a university is referred to as *sōchō* or *gakuchō.*

Bellmeyer: 大統領... ご決断 を
Daitōryō, go-ketsudan o
president (hon-) decision (obj.)
"Mr. President, you need to make a decision."

- the sentence is left unfinished, implying something like *go-ketsuron o (dasanakute wa narimasen)* "You must make/come to a decision."

© Saitō Takao / *Gorugo 13,* Shogakukan

In this scene Hamasaki addresses his company's CEO as *shachō* ("company president"). Although the situation here is confrontational (the employees are trying to negotiate a pay increase), this usage (title only, without his name) is perfectly acceptable and does not imply any lack of respect toward the president.

© Yamasaki & Kitami / *Tsuri-Baka Nisshi,* Shogakukan

Hamasaki:
社長!! 我々 の 要求 に 応えてください!
Shachō!! Wareware no yōkyū ni kotaete kudasai!
(company) president we/us 's demand(s) to respond please
"Sir, please respond to our demands!" (PL3)

President:
そこ を どきなさい!!
Soko o doki-nasai!!
there (obj.) move/get out of the way
"Move aside!!" (PL2)

- *shachō* is "company president/CEO," written with the kanji 社 ("company") and 長 ("head/chief"). Typical corporate structure has the *shachō* at the top, followed by a number of *buchō* ("department/division chiefs") under whom are *kachō* ("section chiefs"). Under *kachō* comes *kakari-chō,* sometimes translated as "sub-section chief."
- *kotaeru* is usually written with the kanji 答える, meaning "answer/reply." Using the kanji 応える implies the broader meaning "respond (to)."
- *doki-nasai* is from the verb *doku* ("get/move out of the way") and the ending *-nasai,* which makes a gentle command.

A title (*kachō*) in place of "you"

Company employees normally utilize titles when speaking of or to those above them, but use informal modes of address with their subordinates. In this scene, everyone in the office had a bit too much to drink the night before, and now they are all suffering from hangovers.

Arima: 課長　　　も？
Kachō　　mo?
section chief also
"Section chief, too?"
"You, too?"

Imanishi: うん... 君 も か ね。
un... kimi mo ka ne.
yeah　　you also (?) (colloq.)
"Uh-huh. Does that mean you, too?" (PL2)

- *un* shows agreement and is an informal "yes."
- *kimi* is an informal/familiar word for "you." It is perfectly natural for a *kachō* (especially an older *kachō*) to use *kimi* to address his subordinates, but the converse would be unthinkable.

© Hayashi & Takai / *Yamaguchi Kakari-chō,* Shogakukan

A title (*kachō*) in place of *-san*

As noted in a previous example (*sensei*), titles can replace the *-san* that would normally come at the end of a name.

Employee: 大野　　課長、　　お車 の 用意　　が できましたが...
Ōno　　kachō, o-kuruma no　yōi　　ga dekimashita ga...
(name) section chief (hon-) car 's preparation (subj.) completed but
"Mr. Ōno, your car is ready ..." (PL3)

Sound FX: カチャ
Kacha
(sound of the latch as the door is opened)

- adding the honorific *o-* to *kuruma* ("car") is a "polite" touch that could be considered a step above PL3 (Ordinary Polite).
- ending a sentence in *ga,* literally "but," softens it by leaving it open to other possibilities. In this example, the *ga* could imply something like, "but (if you're not ready yet it can wait)."

© Kamata Yōji / *Tanburingu* , Futabasha

Other *chō* (-長) titles

The ending *-chō* is used in numerous combinations to indicate the head or person in charge. Here are a few examples.

© Yamasaki & Kitami / *Tsuri-Baka Nisshi*, Shogakukan

Committee member: しかし　委員長。
Shikashi   iinchō.
but   committee chairman
"But Mr. Chairman . . ."

Chairman: ン!?
N!?
"Huh?"

- *iin* means "member of a committee," so *iinchō* is "committee chairman."

Detective:
校長!! あの額の写真
Kōchō!! Ano gaku no shashin
principal that frame's photo

は　誰ですか!?
wa   dare desu ka!?
as for who is (?)
"Sir, who is (the person) in that framed photo?" (PL3)

- *kōchō* (or often *kōchō sensei*) is the title for the principal of a school.

© Nōjō Jun'ichi / *Purinsu*, Shogakukan

© Kunitomo Yasuyuki / *Kikaku Ari*, Shogakukan

Secretary:
会長、　　　　お電話　が 入っておりますが...
Kaichō,   o-denwa   ga   haitte-orimasu   ga...
chairman/director (hon-)phone (subj.)   entered   but
"Director, a call has come in but . . ."
"Sir, there's a call for you." (PL4)

- *kaichō* is the title for a chairman of the board or the director of an association. In a corporate hierarchy, *kaichō* is a step above *shachō*.

Clerk: 店長おぉぅ、たっ、たっ、
Tenchō—   ta–   ta–
store manager   aw–   aw–

大変 ですー!!
taihen desu—!!
awful   is
"Store manager, i- i- it's awful!"
"Mr. Kameyoshi, we- we- we've got a big problem!!" (PL3)

- *tenchō*, written with the kanji for "store" and "head/chief," means "store manager."
- the store manager's name is Kameyoshi.
- the boy's apron reads *kame-sutoā, kame* from the name Kameyoshi plus the katakana version of "store."

© Hoshi Kira / *Konbini Kankei*, Shogakukan

Occupation as a title

Occupations can also be used like titles. In this case, it is "Mr. Driver." (*O*)*kyaku-san* ("[hon.] Mr./Ms. Customer") is also used like a title by the person whose business is being patronized. In this scene, the man has caught a taxi for his girlfriend, and is making sure that the driver treats her courteously during the trip.

© Saimon Fumi / *Asunaro Hakusho*, Shogakukan

運転手さん、大切な　お客さん　なん　だ　から。
Untenshu-san taisetsu-na okyaku-san na n da kara.
driver (-hon)   important (hon-) customer (explan.-) is because
"Driver, this is an important client, so . . ." (PL2)

Senpai

The ***senpai-kōhai*** ("senior-junior") relationship is an important part of the social hierarchy in Japan. In its broadest sense, *senpai* refers to "one who goes before and leads the way" — in a school, the upperclassmen, in a company, those who joined before the *kōhai*/"junior." *Senpai* are something like mentors to those who come after them. The *kōhai* frequently address the seniors as *senpai*, while the seniors would simply address the juniors by their name or with an informal word for "you."

Senior:
とにかく 俺 と　全く 同じようにすれば いいんだ。
Tonikaku ore to mattaku onaji yō ni sureba ii n da.
anyway   I/me to completely same as if do is good
わかった ね?
Wakatta   ne?
understood right
"In any case, you do exactly as I do, understand?"

Junior:
はいっ 先輩!
Hai! Senpai!
"Yes, *senpai*!"

• *ore* is an informal/rough masculine word for "I/me."

© Yamashina Keisuke / *C-kumi Sarariiman Kōza*, Shogakukan

Some other titles

There are far too many titles to illustrate in our limited space, so here is a listing of a few more.

Chōkan	Director, administrator	*Kashira*	Boss, head
Chōrō	Elder	*Keiji/keibu*	Police detective/inspector
Fukushachō	Vice president (of a company)	*Masutā*	Master/proprietor (of a shop)
Jichō	Assistant chief, deputy director	*Senmu*	Managing Director
Kakka	Your excellency	*Shishō*	Master, teacher (of an art)
Kanjichō	Executive Secretary	*Shunin*	Chief, head
Kantoku	Director (of a movie), manager (of a team)	*Sōri*	Prime Minister

Lesson 33 • *Iya*

***Iya* is actually three separate words.** The first *iya* (which can be written with the kanji 嫌) means "disagreeable" or "unpleasant." *Iya desu* (or the shorter and blunter *ya da*), expresses distaste for a thing, idea, or situation. *Iya na* is the adjective form, describing the chosen noun as distasteful, and the verb form, *iyagaru,* means "dislike," or "act as if something were unpleasant/disagreeable."

The second *iya* is an interjection or sort of verbal warm-up, which in itself has no negative implications at all—though it can introduce a negative statement.

The third *iya* means "no," and is a variation or corruption of *iie*, the standard textbook word for "no."

All three words are very common and sure to be heard often in everyday Japanese, as well as seen in print when reading manga or dialog.

Disagreeable/Don't like

Garcia-kun's little neighbor isn't too happy about living next to a *gaikokujin* ("foreigner") whom she thinks looks like a gorilla (namely Garcia), and she lets her mom know it in no uncertain terms.

© Takeuchi Akira / *Garcia-kun*, Futabasha

<u>Girl (off panel)</u>: ママ〜〜 やっぱり この アパート イヤ ダァ〜〜
Mama— yappari kono apāto iya da—
mom of course/after all this apartment disagreeable is
"Mo–o–om, I really do ha–a–ate this apartment!" (PL2)

- *yappari* means "after all/as expected," and in this case implies that some earlier feeling/statement is now (re)-confirmed. (See Basic Japanese No. 27)
- *apāto* is abbreviated from *apātomento*, the cumbersome katakana rendering of the English word "apartment."
- the girl has omitted the topic/subject-marker *wa* that would normally follow *apāto*.

Don't want to

Amuro thought he had a bright future in sumo when he first started training because he easily beat the more experienced wrestlers. He soon found out that they were just letting him win as a way to tease him, and is now depressed. The sumo stable's *okami* ("proprietress"; in the case of a sumo stable, the wife of the owner) is making sure he's OK.

Okami-san: みんな　と　チャンコ　食べない？
Minna　to　chanko　tabenai?
everyone　with　(name of dish)　won't (you) eat

いや　　なら　　帰ってもいい　　けれど。
Iya　nara　kaette mo ii　keredo.
disagreeable　if　is all right to return/go home　but

"Won't you come have some *chanko* with everyone? If you don't want to, it's OK to go home." (PL2)

- *chanko* is a stew-like dish consisting of seafood, meat, and vegetables in a broth. It is the traditional food of sumo wrestlers, and is supposed to help them put on weight.
- ending a sentence in *keredo* (lit. "but") softens it by leaving it open to other possibilities.

Refusal

At age fifteen, Amuro has quit school to train as a sumo wrestler. His school counselor, Ms. Nakagawa, has been trying to convince him to at least finish high school while continuing his training at a less vigorous pace. To show her that sumo is the right thing for him, Amuro asks her to come watch him in practice, and arranges to have an opponent throw the match so he'll look good. The idea backfires when his opponent doesn't follow the plan and clobbers him mercilessly. Although we have translated *iya* as "no" in this and the following example, these usages still have the feeling of "disagreeable" and are not examples of *iya* as a replacement for *iie* ("no").

© Ichimaru / *Okami-san*, Shogakukan

Nakagawa: 先生、　　やっぱり　　　進学
Sensei,　yappari　shingaku
teacher/I　of course/after all　advance in school

した方がいい　　と　思う　わ。
shita hō ga ii　to　omou　wa.
would be better to　(quote)　think (fem. colloq.)

"I really think that you'd do better to stay in school." (PL2)

Amuro: いや　　です。　／　今日　は、　たまたま
Iya　desu.　/　Kyō　wa,　tama tama
disagreeable　is　today　as for　by chance

調子　　が　悪かった　だけ　なん　だ　から。
chōshi　ga　warukatta　dake　nan　da　kara.
condition　(subj.)　was bad　only　(explan.)　is　because

"No, I don't want to. I just happened to be off today." (PL3; PL2)

- Nakagawa is referring to herself when she says *sensei*, a fact that is not obvious without context. She has left out the topic marker *wa* that would normally follow *sensei*.
- . . . *-ta hō ga ii* is a pattern meaning "it would be better to . . ."

Distasteful

Mrs. Suzumoto is having complications with her pregnancy, and is worried that the treatment for her will kill the unborn baby. As was the case in the previous example, this usage of *iya* can be translated as "no," but it is still *iya* in the sense of "disagreeable/unpleasant," (somewhat stronger here). The *iya* which is an equivalent of *iie* ("no") is shown in the last example.

© Nōjō Jun'ichi / *Gekka no Kishi*, Shogakukan

Suzumoto: いや　　　　　　よ!!　　　向こう　　へ　行って!!
Iya　　　　　　*yo!!*　　　*Mukō*　　*e*　*itte!!*
abhorrent/unwelcome (emph.)　other side/over there　to　(please) go
"No! Go over there!"
"No! Get away from me!" (PL2)

いや!!　　いや!!　赤ちゃん を、殺さないで!!
Iya!!　　*Iya!!*　*Akachan o,*　*korosanaide!!*
abhorrent　abhorrent　baby　(obj.)　(please) don't kill
"No! No! Please don't kill the baby!" (PL2)

- in both sentences, the *-te/-de* form of a verb is used as a strong request, more like a command in this case. Adding *kudasai* (see below) makes a polite request.

Forget it

This man's job has prestige, high pay, and plenty of vacation time, but he has just finished explaining to his friend that he still feels there is some job out there better suited to him. Garcia's job has none of those things, so he gladly offers to trade places with the man.

© Takeuchi Akira / *Garcia-kun*, Futabasha

Garcia: じゃ、代って 下さい。
Ja, kawatte kudasai.
well　exchange　please
"Well then, let's trade."
(PL3)

Man: や　　　だ　よ。
Ya　　*da*　*yo.*
disagreeable　is　(emph.)
"Forget it." (PL2)

- shortening *iya da* to *ya da* is quite common.
- the plain form *da* and the emphatic *yo* make the refusal blunt.

Iya as a modifier

Adding -*na* to *iya* makes it a modifier. In this scene, Kyōko, who has fought a humbling bout with a malignant tumor, is thinking back about the way she used to act when she was more carefree but also selfish and irresponsible. She used to try to get admirers to do silly or dangerous things and delighted in humiliating people and then laughing at them.

Kyōko: 嫌な　　女　だった　わ。
Iya na　onna　datta　wa.
distasteful　woman　was　(fem. colloq.)
"I was a horrible woman."
(PL2)

Iya ni naru

Literally "become distasteful," *iya ni naru* means "come to dislike/grow tired of." In this story, a man is explaining that he loves his wife so much that he wants to offer to find her a better mate. He is willing to make this sacrifice for her happiness, but realizes that she'd take it the wrong way.

© Nakazaki Tatsuya / *Jimihen*, Shogakukan

Wife: 私　　が　イヤになった　　の　ね。
Watashi ga　iya ni natta　no　ne.
I/me　(subj.)　became distasteful　(explan.) (colloq.)
"You're tired of me, aren't you." (PL2)

それとも　他に　好きな人　が
Sore tomo hoka ni suki na hito ga
or is it　in addition　liked person　(subj.)

できた　　　の?
dekita　　no?
came into existence　(?)
"Or is it that you've found someone else you like?" (PL2)

Narration: なんて　誤解する　　だろう。
Nante　gokai suru　darō.
(quote)　misunderstand　probably/surely
She'd probably misunderstand it as something like that. (PL2)

- *dekita* is the plain past form of *dekiru* ("can/finish/make"), and can be used like the "make" in the English expression "make a friend."
- in this usage *nante* is a colloquial *nado to*, ("things like" + quotative *to*), indicating that the preceding "quote" is how his wife would misunderstand.

A light-hearted response

***Iya (da)* can be used for feigned displeasure** in situations where you are not really offended. In this example, Aki's father, who still treats her like a young girl, wants her to come sit on his lap. She has a visitor, so she is a touch embarrassed at the way her father treats her, although she isn't really upset.

© Akiyama Jōji / *Haguregumo*, Shogakukan

Father: はい、お秋ちゃん　いらっしゃい。
Hai,　O-Aki-chan　irasshai
yes/OK　(name)　come
"OK, O-Aki-chan, come here." (PL3-4)

Aki: や　だあ、お友達　が　いる　のに。
Ya　da–, o-tomodachi　ga　iru　no ni.
disagreeable is　(hon.)- friend (subj.)　is here even though
"Oh, stop it! I have a friend here!" (PL2)

- *irasshai* is a polite way to ask someone to come along or to come to where the speaker is. Parents frequently use polite speech forms when speaking to small children.
- adding the honorific *o-* to a girl's name is an old-fashioned touch that indicates a sense of familiarity.
- extending the *da* in *(i)ya da* adds emphasis.

We don't know exactly what Mr. Ogawa has just told Miss Onuki, but we can tell by her reaction that she is amused, even though she says *(i)ya da*.

Onuki: や　だーっ
Ya　da—!
disgusting is
"Oh, yu-u-uk!" (PL2)

Ogawa: ほんとほんと　ハハハハ
Honto　honto　ha ha ha ha
really　really　(laugh)
"It's true, it's true (laugh)." (PL2)

- *honto* is a colloquial *hontō* ("real/true").

© Deguchi & Minagawa / *Manga Bijinesu Manā*, Sunmark

Iya as an interjection

As a verbal "warm-up," *iya* has no particular meaning and is simply used like "Well," "You know," or a variety of other interjections in English. Such usage is illustrated in this scene, where Shōsuke and his supervisor Takeshita have taken a business trip to Thailand, hoping to find some food products made from Thai rice that would appeal to Japanese consumers. They have made a stop in a Thai Chinatown.

© Hijiri Hideo / *Dakara Shōsuke,* Shogakukan

Shōsuke:
いやあ　おいしい　です　よ。
Iya-　oishii　desu　yo.
well/you know　delicious　is　(emph.)
"Ahh, this is good." (PL3)

Takeshita:
さすが、チャイナタウンの　朝がゆ　です　ね。
Sasuga　Chainataun　no asa-gayu desu　ne.
as expected　Chinatown　's (name of dish) is (colloq.)
"As you'd expect of Chinatown's *asa-gayu.*" (PL3)

- *asa-gayu* is from *asa* ("morning") and *kayu* ("gruel;" the *ka* changes to *ga* for euphony). (*O*)*kayu* is rice cooked with more water than regular steamed rice, so that it has a soupy consistency. In Japan, *okayu* is usually associated with being ill—something like chicken soup in the US. In China, however, *asa-gayu* (lit. "morning *kayu*") is apparently a common breakfast food, without the "chicken soup" image. We have heard that this Chinese breakfast has recently achieved trendy status among young Japanese people.

Iya = No

This is an example of the *iya* which is a variation or corruption of the word *iie* ("no"). Kōsuke has elevated cheap living to an art form, and he makes full use of the belongings of the student next door. His girlfriend has cooked him a spaghetti dinner, and now he is giving her a ride to the train station, using his neighbor's bicycle.

© Maekawa Tsukasa / *Dai-Tōkyō Binbō Seikatsu Manyuaru,* Kodansha

Hiroko: これ あなた の 自転車?
Kore　anata　no　jitensha?
this　you　's　bicycle
"Is this your bicycle?" (PL2)

Kōsuke: いや...
Iya...
no
"Nope..." (PL2)

Sign: 平和荘
Heiwa-Sō
Peace Villa

- Hiroko has left out the topic/subject marker *wa* that would normally follow *kore.*
- Kōsuke is a man of few words, and this terse response is not typical usage. Most people would offer an explanation after *iya.*
- the suffix *-sō* is commonly used in the names of apartment buildings (usually Japanese-style). It's also used in compounds to mean "house/cottage" (*bessō* = "a second house in the country").

BASIC JAPANESE through comics

Lesson 34 • *Daijōbu*

Students usually learn *daijōbu* as the Japanese equivalent of "all right," and indeed, it is possible to use it in many of the same ways as the English phrase. But beginners tend to overuse *daijōbu*, carrying it over into situations where a native speaker would never use the word.

One clue to the meaning of *daijōbu* is in the kanji used to write it: 大丈夫. The last two kanji can be used by themselves to write *jōbu*, meaning "sturdiness," or "good health/strong physical condition," and one of the basic meanings of *daijōbu* is "all right in a physical sense/unharmed." From this, the meaning has expanded to more abstract or psychological meanings such as "nothing to worry about," "reliable," "able to handle the situation," "certain to come out well," and "convenient/feasible," all of which can be expressed with a simple "all right" in English. In other words, in any situation where you could say *daijōbu* in Japanese, you could also say "all right" in English. The reverse, however, is not true.

Native speakers of English should avoid using *daijōbu* the way they're accustomed to using "all right" in English, as an all-purpose expression of approval, acknowledgment, or consent. For example, if you were asked in English for your opinion of a mildly entertaining but mostly forgettable movie, you might answer, "It was all right." In Japanese, you would never say *Daijōbu deshita* but rather *Māmā deshita* ("it was so-so"). Similarly, if your boss told you that the meeting was starting in five minutes, in English you might say, "all right," but in Japanese you need to say something like *Wakarimashita. [Sugu mairimasu]* ("I understand. [I'll be there right away]"). *Daijōbu* also does not work as an exclamation of joy, "All *right*!" The correct word in this case is *Yatta!* (covered in Basic Japanese No. 13).

As usual, the best way to get a feel for the range of the word is to look at some real examples.

"All right" in a physical sense

An exhausted "salaryman" is on a business trip and has been working three days straight on materials needed to close a deal with an important client. His trip was only supposed to last one day, but everything seemed to go wrong: he couldn't concentrate because his cheap hotel was close to noisy railroad tracks, he lost track of time and missed an appointment, and he misplaced a crucial report. Ready to give up, he arrives at the upscale Hotel Platon, but before he can even check in, he collapses into the arms of Tōdō, the hotel manager.

<u>Tōdō:</u> 大丈夫 です か。
Daijōbu desu ka.
all right   are   (?)
"Are you all right?" (PL3)

<u>Salaryman:</u> す...すみません...
Su. . . sumimasen
"I . . . I'm sorry." (PL3)

• in this situation, *sumimasen* also carries a strong implication of its other meaning, "thank you."

© Ishinomori Shōtarō / *Hotel*, Shogakukan

True to form, the self-centered Obatarian fakes a sudden attack of stomach trouble so the bus driver will let her off right in front of her house instead of at the designated stop.

Obatarian: 運転手さん、と・とめて、苦し～。
Untenshu-san,   to- tomete.   Kurushii.
Driver (-hon)   stop   agonizing
"Driver, s-stop! I'm in pain." (PL2)

Driver: 大丈夫 です か。
Daijōbu desu ka?
all right   are   (?)
"Are you all right?" (PL3)

Sound FX: キッ
Ki!
(a short squeak/screech from suddenly hitting the brakes)

• *kurushii* connotes extreme suffering or difficulty in carrying on. For example, a person having a heart attack might complain *Iki ga kurushii,* "I'm having trouble breathing."

© Hotta Katsuhiko/ *Obatarian,* Take Shobo

Bau, the stray dog, has just jumped out of a car window and landed on his head on the pavement. Inugami, whose house Bau has recently been hanging around, happens by at this point.

© Terii Yamamoto / *Bau,* Shogakukan

Policeman: おい、ワン公、大丈夫 か?
Oi,   Wankō,   daijōbu ka?
hey   (dog -fam.) all right (?)
"Hey, pooch, are you all right?" (PL2)

Sound FX: ピク ピク
Piku piku
(twitching effect—here of involuntary muscle spasms after being knocked unconscious)

Inugami: ほー   その 駄犬 と   知り合い な の かい。
Ho–,   sono daken to   shiriai na no kai.
(exclamation) that   mutt with acquaintance is (explan.) (?)
"Huh? Do you know that mongrel?"

• the sound FX for a dog's barking is *wanwan,* and *wan* is used in a number of colloquial terms for dogs, such as *wan-chan,* a child's word for "puppy/doggy." *Wankō* is another such "generic" term for "dog," and has a feeling of familiarity when used to address a dog directly. In some cases, the ending *-kō* can be derogatory; for example, *senkō* is a derisive term for "teacher," and *porikō* is a rough, masculine word for "policeman."
• Inugami's name (犬神) is written with kanji meaning "dog god."

Not a cause for concern

Kōsuke and his girlfriend Hiroko are out drinking. Kōsuke's usual limit is one drink.

© Maekawa Tsukasa / *Dai-Tōkyō Binbō Seikatsu Manyuaru*, Kodansha

Narration: 久し振りに　飲んだ　リザーブ　は　　やはり　　ウマかった ので、おかわり　をしてしまった。
Hisashiburi ni nonda Rizābu wa yahari umakatta node, okawari o shite shimatta.
after a long time　drank　(name of whiskey)　as for　as would expect　was delicious　because　refill/seconds (obj.)　ended up doing
The (Suntory) Reserve, which I was drinking for the first time in a long time, was really good, so I ended up getting a refill. (PL2)

Kōsuke: おかわり。
Okawari.
(hon.) replacement
"Another." (PL2)

Hiroko: だいじょーぶ?
Daijōbu?
"(Will you be) all right?" (PL2)

• *hisashiburi* refers to a long time/absence. (*Hisashiburi desu,* "it's been a long time," is often used as a greeting when meeting old friends whom you haven't seen in a while.) We also considered ". . . (the) Reserve, which I hadn't had in a long time, . . ." as a translation for *hisashiburi ni nonda Rizābu.*
• *shimatta* after the *-te* form of a verb can mean the action was done even though the person knew better.
• *okawari* is essentially a noun form of *kawaru* ("change/be replaced"). The honorific prefix *o-* is always necessary for the meaning of "seconds/a refill."

A young woman has been kidnapped, and the two kidnappers have just brought her to their hideout.

© Inose & Hirokane / *Rasuto Nyūsu*, Shogakukan

Kidnapper: 大丈夫 だ、おまえ は　大事な　人質　だ。
Daijōbu da, omae wa daiji-na hitojichi da.
all right　is　you　as for　valuable　hostage　are.
おとなしくしていれば、殺したり　は　しない。
Otonashiku shite ireba, koroshitari wa shinai.
if behave well/keep quiet　things like killing　as for　won't do
"Don't worry. You're a valuable hostage. As long as you behave yourself, we won't kill you or anything." (PL2)

• *otonashiku* is the adverb form of *otonashii,* "quiet/well behaved." *Shite ireba* is the conditional ("if") form of *shite iru,* "are doing." Together they mean "if (you are) quiet/well behaved . . ."
• the *-tari* form of a verb, usually followed by a form of *suru* (*shinai* is negative of *suru*), implies the action is one of several possible actions: "do things like 〜" → "do something/anything like 〜"

The two women are visiting the young man when a mouse comes out of a hole in the wall. As it turns out, the mouse performs the useful function of killing cockroaches.

© Ueda Masashi / *Kariage-kun*, Futabasha

Man: だいじょうぶ、だいじょうぶ。味方 だ から。
Daijōbu,   daijōbu.   Mikata da kara.
all right   all right   ally   is because
"It's OK, it's OK. He's on our side." (PL2)

Woman: なに が 味方 よ。ねずみ は ねずみ よ。
Nani ga mikata yo.   Nezumi wa nezumi yo.
What (subj.) ally (emph.) mouse/rat as for mouse/rat (emph.)
"What do you mean, 'on our side'? A mouse is a mouse!" (PL2)

- the lines in the dialog box that look like extended くs are re-peat lines, indicating that he said *daijōbu* twice.
- *nezumi* can refer to a mouse or a rat, although the word *hatsuka-nezumi* (lit. "20-day mouse/rat") refers specifically to a mouse.

Reliable, trustworthy

Mrs. Barnum is worried about her tenant, a university researcher named Annabel Johnson, who has disappeared. To look for clues, she takes Keaton, an archaeology professor and part-time investigator, along to the university where Annabel has been working. Their cover story is that Mrs. Barnum has Keaton in mind as a potential husband for Annabel. Just before this frame, the laboratory supervisor has mentioned that Annabel's previous husband was no good and had affairs with a lot of other women.

Mrs. Barnum:
え...ええ、でも、その 点、この キートンさん は
E...ē,   demo, sono ten, kono Kiiton-san wa
y-yes   however that point this (name -hon) as for
大丈夫、 私 が 保証します わ。
daijōbu, watashi ga hoshō shimasu wa.
all right, I (subj.) assure/guarantee (fem. colloq.)
"Y-yes, however, in that regard, Mr. Keaton is all right. I guarantee it." (PL3)

愛人 を 作る なんて 器用な こと が できる
Aijin o tsukuru nante kiyō na koto ga dekiru
lover (obj.) make/find (quote) clever thing (subj.) can do
わけ が ありません もの。
wake ga arimasen mono.
situation (subj) does not exist because
"There's no way he'd be able to do something clever like getting himself a lover." (PL3)

© Katsushika & Urasawa / *Mastā Kiiton*, Shogakukan

- *nanka* is a colloquial quotative form that implies the preceding is "ridiculous/out of the question."
- *kiyō-na* = "clever/dexterous," but here it's being used ironically.

Can handle it (psychologically)

The young man has two girlfriends, and he has finally decided which one to marry. Although the rejected girlfriend is upset at first, she finally realizes that anyone stupid enough to marry her rival isn't worth having.

Young Man:
ごめん。君 は 一人 でも 大丈夫 だけど
Gomen. Kimi wa hitori demo daijōbu da kedo
I'm sorry you as for alone even all right are but

典子 は オレ が いない と...
Noriko wa ore ga inai to...
Noriko as for I (subj.) not there if/when
"I'm sorry. You'll be fine by yourself, but Noriko— without me . . ." (PL2)

典子 と 結婚 する。
Noriko to kekkon suru.
Noriko with marriage do.
"I'm going to marry Noriko." (PL2)

Girl Friend:
そんな...
Sonna . . .
that kind of
"What a thing to say."

- *sonna* is a common expression of dismay or protest. Depending on the situation and the speaker's tone of voice, it can mean anything from "No, that can't be!" to "How dare you!"

© Nakazaki Tatsuya / *Jimihen*, Shogakukan

This young man is a studying to become a barber, but he has done terribly during the class sessions, even slicing off the head of a practice dummy in one case. Now he is going to shave his first real live customer.

© Fujiko Fujio (A) / *Warau Sērusuman*, Chuo Koronsha

Teacher: ほ、ほんとに 大丈夫 か。
Ho-honto ni daijōbu ka.
truly all right (?)
"Are you sure you're all right?" (PL2)

Customer: お-おい、おい! 大丈夫 か と は どんな こと なん だ?
O-oi, oi! Daijōbu ka to wa donna koto nan da?
h-hey, hey! all right (?) (quote) as for what kind of thing (explan.) is
"Wait a minute! What do you mean, 'Are you all right'?" (PL2)

- in this case, the meaning of *daijōbu* is somewhat ambiguous, hence the customer's question.

Convenient or feasible

The man pictured here has a crush on Ms. Fujiki, the manager of his department, but in this frame, he is taking a message from a male caller who wants to go to dinner with her that evening. The man tells the caller that Ms. Fujiki is free, even though he knows that she has a previous appointment.

Man: は、大丈夫 だ と 思います。では、そのように
Ha, daijōbu da to omoimasu. Dewa, sono yō ni
yes all right is (quote) think well in that way

伝えておきます。 はい、どーも、それでは...
tsutaete-okimasu. Hai, dōmo, sore de wa...
convey (ahead of time) yes thank you well then

"Yes, I think it'll be all right. Well, I'll give her the message. Yes, thank you. Well, then . . ." (PL3)

• *tsutaete-okimasu* is the PL3 form of *tsutaete-oku*, from *tsutaeru*, "tell/convey." The *-te oku* form means that something is done "in preparation" or "for some future purpose," implying that some other (related) action (or reaction) will follow. In this example, it implies "I'll give her the message, but I don't know what she will do."

• *dōmo* is a polite, all-purpose word meaning "indeed/really/quite," and is often used as a shortened form of *dōmo arigatō gozaimasu* to mean "thank you." In this case, it's just a formulaic part of ending a phone conversation. It's actually the other party who should be saying "thank you."

Hasegawa, a professional golfer, has just told this woman that he will be waiting for her that night in the usual place.

Woman: 今夜...
Kon'ya...
"Tonight?" (PL2)

Hasegawa: まずい の か?
Mazui no ka?
bad/awkward (explan.) (?)
"Is it awkward for you?" (PL2)

Woman: ううん、大丈夫、待ってる わ。
Uun, daijōbu, matte-ru wa.
uh-uh all right am waiting (fem. colloq.)
"Uh-uh. It's all right. I'll be waiting." (PL2)

• students usually learn *mazui* first in the sense of "bad-tasting," but it has a number of other meanings, including "awkward," "unwise," and "poorly handled."

• *uun*, said with a rising, then falling intonation, is a very informal way to say "no." The corresponding equivalent of "yeah" is a short *un*, spoken almost like a grunt.

Lesson 35 • *Mono* (Part 1)

***Mono* is another one of those words** that seem like they should be so easy to use and understand. After all, its basic meaning is simply "thing." In reality, though, *mono* (often shortened to *mon*) isn't just one word with one meaning. Beyond the easily comprehended noun *mono* is a more vague particle *mono*, which adds emphasis or indicates that an explanation is being offered. There are also many idiomatic usages and phrases that incorporate *mono,* some of which we will cover in the next installment of *Basic Japanese.*

All in all, *mono* is probably one of the most-used words in the Japanese language, and while none of the meanings is really too hard to understand, the wide range of usages may make it difficult to get a firm grasp on it at first. The following manga examples should help you begin to sort out the different uses and give you some insight into the use of *mono* in real-world Japanese. Then, the next time someone tries to tell you that the language is incomprehensible, you can say, *"Chigau mon!"* ("That's not so!")

Mono = "person"

When written with the kanji 者, *mono* means "person." Here Sakamoto Seizō is trying to track down his older brother Keikichi in order to convince him to go back to live with his son. Seizō has found the neighborhood where Keikichi lives, so he inquires about his brother to a man on the street.
  者 is the humble counterpart of (人) *hito* or (方) *kata*. Seizō uses it because he is referring to a member of his own family.

© Utsumi & Taniguchi / *Hitobito Shiriizu,* Shogakukan

Seizō: ここ に、 坂本 と いう 者 が いる でしょう か?
Koko ni, Sakamoto to iu mono ga iru deshō ka?
here at (name) called person (subj.) exist(s) (?)
"Is there someone named Sakamoto around here?"
"Does someone named Sakamoto live around here?" (PL3)

• *deshō* by itself usually seeks agreement ("right?") or sometimes means "probably is," but when used with the question indicator *ka,* it is really just a polite way of asking, "is it?/does it?," so *iru deshō ka* = "does he exist/is he present?"

Mono = "physical thing"

These two amateur sumo wrestlers have been practicing their moves for a rigged match the next day. After his ladyfriend makes a disparaging remark, Date no Yama offers Take'emon some *mitarashi dango* (a type of rice-ball dumpling) as a token of apology. Take'emon's response also demonstrates how *mono* is sometimes contracted to *mon*.

© Sakurai Toshifumi / *Ushimatagi Take'emon*, Futabasha

Date no Yama:
すみません 武さん。つまんない もの ですが、
Sumimasen Take-san. Tsumannai mono desu ga,
sorry/excuse me (name -hon) trifling thing is but
これ でも 食べて機嫌 なおしてください。
kore demo tabete kigen naoshite kudasai.
this or something eat mood fix please
"Sorry, Take-san. It's a trifling thing, but please eat something like this and fix your mood."
"Sorry, Take-san. It's really nothing, but maybe these will help you feel better." (PL3)

Take'emon:
みたらし団子 か。ほんとに つまんないもんだ ねー。
Mitarashi dango ka. Honto ni tsumannai mon da nē.
(type of rice dumpling) (?) really/truly trifling thing is (colloq.)
"*Mitarashi dango*, is it? It really is a trifling thing, isn't it."
"*Mitarashi dango*, huh? You aren't kidding when you say it's nothing." (PL2)

- *tsumannai* is a colloquial contraction of *tsumaranai*, "trifling/dull."
- adding *demo*, "something like," when making a suggestion softens it by implying that there are other possible options.
- *dango* are steamed or boiled dumplings made from rice flour. *Mitarashi dango* are a type of *dango* that originated in Kyōto, served with a syrupy mixture of soy sauce and sugar.

Mono = "abstract thing"

Even though the artist is an important business client, Tsuchii's admiration for the painting seems to be genuine.

© Yamasaki & Kitami / *Tsuri-Baka Nisshi*, Shogakukan

Tsuchii: でも 確実に 私 の 心 に
Demo kakujitsu-ni watashi no kokoro ni
but certainly I/me 's heart to
伝わってくる もの が あります。
tsutawatte-kuru mono ga arimasu.
is conveyed/transmitted-and comes thing (subj.) exists
"But there's something that's definitely transmitted to my heart."
"But there's something here that really touches my heart." (PL3)

Indicating a tendency/characteristic

Generalizations can be expressed with *mono,* coming across as something like ". . . are things that . . ." Here Garcia-kun has brought the kindergarten terror Crayon Shin-chan (who is visiting from another manga title in *Action Comics*) to the local pool, and one of the parents thinks Shin-chan is setting a bad example. She wants Garcia to do something about it, but Garcia's attitude is pretty laid-back.

© Takeuchi Akira / *Garcia-kun,* Futabasha

Parent: のん気な こと 言って　ケガ人出たら アナタの せい　よ。
Nonki-na koto itte keganin detara anata no sei yo.
carefree thing say-and if someone is injured your fault (emph.)
"With such a carefree attitude, it'll be your fault if some-one gets hurt." (PL2)

Garcia: 子供　は 気をつけても ケガする もの です。
Kodomo wa ki o tsukete mo kega suru mono desu.
children as-for even if are careful get injured thing is/are
"As for children, even if you're careful they are things that get injured."
"No matter how careful you are, kids have a way of getting hurt." (PL3)

- *nonki-na* means "carefree/laid-back" and *nonki-na koto o itte* is a continuing form of *nonki-na koto o iu* ("say carefree/easy things.")
- *keganin (ga) detara* is a conditional ("if") form of *keganin (ga) deru,* literally "an injured person appears" → "someone gets injured."

Past tendency

The use of *mono* to describe tendencies is not limited to just the present. *Mon(o) da* after a past tense verb means "used to (do the action)/always (did/have done the action)." This old lady has sneaked off from her family's store to play pachinko. When someone comes to tell her that things are busy and they need her back at the store, she recalls how things were back when *she* was in charge.

© Maekawa Tsukasa / *Dai-Tōkyō Binbō Seikatsu Manyuaru,* Kodansha

あたしなんか　どんなに　忙しくても　ひとりで　きりもりして　きたもん　だがねえ!

Yukari: あたし なんか　　どんなに　　忙しくても
Atashi nannka donna-ni isogashikute mo
I/me someone like no matter how much even if busy

ひとりで　　きりもりしてきたもん だ が ねえ!
hitori de kirimori shite kita mon da ga nē!
alone/by myself managed-and-came thing is but (colloq.)
"I always managed by myself no matter how busy things got!" (PL2)

- *nanka* can stand in place of the topic marker *wa* ("as for"), often with a belittling/critical feeling toward the topic, but in this case it just emphasizes *atashi* ("I/me").
- *isogashikute mo* is from *isogashii* ("busy"). The *-te mo* form means "even if/when 〜"
- *kirimori shite* is the *-te* form of *kirimori suru* ("manage/administer"). *Kita* is the plain/abrupt past form of *kuru* ("come"), here implying the action started sometime in the past and continues to the present → "I've always 〜"

Should/shouldn't

Following the present form of a verb, *mon(o) da* can also mean, "should/must (do the action)." The setting for this scene is a hotel where a medical convention is being held. One of the hotel guests isn't feeling well, and since the regular hotel doctor is unavailable, the visiting Dr. Shibata volunteers to examine him. It turns out that the man has a touch of the flu, so Shibata tells him to go home and get some rest. When the patient explains that he's from out of town on important business that simply must be completed, the doctor gets a bit irate.

© Ishinomori Shōtarō / *Hotel*, Shogakukan

Dr. Shibata: 患者　は　医者の言う事　を　聞くもんだ!
Kanja wa isha no iu koto o kiku mon da!
patient as for what the doctor says (obj.) should listen to/heed
"A patient should do as his doctor says." (PL2)

そう　でなければ　いつまでたっても　治らん　ぞ!
Sō de nakereba itsu made tatte mo naoran zo!
that way if is not forever won't get better (emph.)
"If you don't, you'll never get better!" (PL2)

- *kiku* literally means "listen to," but in this usage it has the idiomatic meaning of "obey/do as (one) says."
- *itsu made tatte mo* is followed by a negative to mean "(something won't happen) no matter how much time passes" → "will never happen."

Otto left his wife and daughter in East Germany 10 years ago when he had a chance to go make his fortune abroad. Now when he comes back for them, he finds that they had to go west to look for work, along with many of the other townspeople. He stops to talk to this old woman, who laments the fact that things have been rough since the Berlin Wall came down.

Old Woman: あーあ、長生きする もんじゃない
Ā–a, naga-iki suru mon ja nai ne.
(sigh) live a long time shouldn't (colloq.)
"I guess a person really shouldn't live so long." (PL2)

ろく　でもない　話　ばっかり だ。
Roku demo nai hanashi bakkari da.
good/decent is not talk nothing but is
"You don't hear anything but bad news." (PL2)

- *roku (-na)* means "good/decent," but is usually used with a negative (*demo nai* in this case) to mean "no good ～ /no decent ～" We also considered translating *roku demo nai hanashi* as "sad stories."
- *bakkari* is a colloquial variation of *bakari*, "only/nothing but."
- *Ā–a* is a drawn-out sigh of disappointment, said with a falling intonation on the long *ā*, then rising quickly on the final *a*.

© Katsushika & Urasawa / *Masutā Kīton*, Shogakukan

Reason/cause

***Mono* can indicate a cause or reason** when giving an explanation. Mrs. Barnum is worried about a university researcher named Annabel Johnson, who has disappeared. Pretending to be Annabel's aunt, she takes Keaton, an archaeology professor and part-time investigator, along to look for clues. Keaton is surprised when she shows him the key to Annabel's apartment, which she procured from the landlord.

© Katsushika & Urasawa / *Mastā Kiiton*, Shogakukan

Mrs. Barnum: なにしろ 私、 彼女の 叔母さんですもの。
nanishiro watashi, kanojo no obasan desu mono.
anyhow I/me   her   aunt is/am because
"After all, I *am* her aunt." (PL3)

Keaton: あ、 ちょっと...
A, chotto...
hey a little
"Hey, wait a sec . . ." (PL2-3)

- *nanishiro* means "at any rate/anyhow/after all/you know."
- the age distinction, i.e. older or younger, is always made when speaking of a person's siblings in Japanese. This distinction carries over to aunts and uncles as well. Although most typically written in hiragana, there are two ways to write the word "aunt" in kanji: 伯母 and 叔母, both pronounced *oba*. The first refers to a parent's older sister, and the second indicates a parent's younger sister. Mrs. Barnum uses 叔母, which shows that she is (pretending to be) Annabel's mother's/father's younger sister, although in spoken language the distinction is lost because the pronunciation is the same. The word "uncle" is also written two ways, 伯父 and 叔父, both pronounced *oji*, referring to a parent's older and younger brother, respectively.

This couple is watching TV, and the wife tells her husband that she has been told she bears a resemblance to the actress on the show. He replies that the actress looks like she has a nasty disposition. The wife continues the conversation . . .

Wife: それで ね、 口元 なんか もう そっくり って!
Sore de ne, kuchimoto nanka mō sokkuri tte
and then (colloq.) mouth area as for (emph.) exactly like (quote)
"So anyway, they say that my mouth is exactly like hers."
(PL2)

Husband: よくしゃべる もん なぁー。
Yoku shaberu mon nā.
a lot talk/speak because (colloq.)
"Because you talk a lot, huh." (PL2)

- *kuchimoto* literally means "mouth area/around the mouth" but in this case can simply be translated as "mouth."
- *nanka* is sometimes used in place of *wa* to mark the topic. It often has a belittling tone but here is just a colloquial usage.

© Naminami Kanko / *Masachūsettsu*, Shogakukan

Emphasis/explanation

As a sentence-ending particle, *mon(o)* can add emphasis to a statement or explanation, with the feel of "(because) that's the way it is." The old man in this scene, Kanamori, is a successful company president. His will to go on has faded, though, and he is now starting to give away his personal possessions. He explains that he has already accomplished all of the things that he wanted to do in life, and thanks Roppeita for having been his friend.

© Hayashi & Takai / *Yamaguchi Roppeita*, Shogakukan

<u>**Roppeita:**</u> なんだい ジジくさい こと 言っちゃって！
nandai   jiji-kusai   koto   itchatte!
why   old-mannish thing   say (regret)
"What do you mean by saying such an old-geezer thing?" (PL2)

<u>**Sound FX:**</u> ガポ
Gapo
Gulp

<u>**Kanamori:**</u> だって ジジイ だ もの。
Datte   jijii   da   mono.
but   old man is/am (explan.)
"But I *am* an old geezer." (PL2)

- *nandai* is a softer form of *nan da*, a blunt "what/why."
- *jiji(i)* is a somewhat derogatory word for "old man." Adding -*kusai*, lit. "stinky," to a noun or adjective forms an adjective that describes something as having the negative aspects of the original word. For example, *mendō-kusai*, = "troublesome/tiresome" (from *mendō*, "trouble"), and *furu-kusai* = "outdated/old fashioned" (from *furui*, "old").
- *itchatte* is a colloquial form of *itte shimatte*, from *iu*, "say." The -*te shimau* form implies that the action is regrettable or inappropriate.

Denial

The emphatic particle *mon(o)* is often used in sentences of denial. To save a little money on food, Yawara has made herself a lunch to take to work. She's trying to save up to go visit her boyfriend, who's on assignment in America, but her nosy grandfather assumes that she wants the extra money to buy fancy clothes and go out dancing.

<u>**Yawara:**</u> ちがう もん。
Chigau   mon.
different (emph/explan.)
"That's not so." (PL2)

旅行 の 費用 ためる ん だ もん。
ryokō no hiyō   tameru   n   da mon.
trip   's expense save/collect (explan.) is (emph.)
"I'm saving money for traveling expenses." (PL2)

<u>**Grandfather:**</u> 旅費ィ？
Ryohii?
"Traveling expenses?" (PL2)

- she has left out the object marker *o* that would normally follow *hiyō*.

© Urusawa Naoki / *Yawara!*, Shogakukan

Lesson 36 • *Mono* (Part 2)

In part 1 we presented examples of the word *mono* used to mean "person" or "thing," to add emphasis, and to indicate that an explanation is being offered. This time we'll explore how *mono* is used in combinations and idioms, but the full range of *mono*'s usage is wide, and our coverage is by no means exhaustive. We found more uses in our manga searches than we could hope to illustrate even in several installments, but with these lessons as a start, you should be able to catch on to the other uses of *mono* as they come up. If you'd like more sources to enhance your understanding, the following should be helpful:

- *A Handbook of Japanese Usage,* by Francis G. Drohan (Tuttle, 1991).
- *All About Particles,* by Naoko Chino (Kodansha, 1991).
- Any comprehensive J-E dictionary. We use *Kenkyusha's New Japanese-English Dictionary* here at *Mangajin* headquarters. It provides a good selection of the idiomatic uses of *mono*, although the Japanese examples are given with no rōmaji or furigana.

Mono in combinations: *Tabemono* = "Food"

***Mono* sometimes combines with verb stems** to form nouns. Two of the most common examples are *tabemono* ("food"), from *taberu* ("eat"), and *nomimono* ("[a] drink"), from *nomu* ("drink"). The girl in this scene from *Yawara!* has been on a diet, but can't take it anymore.

Girl: お願い ... / なにか 食べ物 を ...
Onegai ... / *nanika tabemono   o*
please   something food   (obj.)
"Please . . . (give me) something to eat . . ."
(PL2-3)

- her sentence is left unfinished, implying something like *nanika tabemono o (kudasai)*.

© Urusawa Naoki / *Yawara!,* Shogakukan

Nomimono = "Beverage"

Natori has just found out that he failed his college entrance exam, so Izumi takes him out to drink and forget.

Waiter: お飲みもの は?
O-nomimono wa?
(hon.-) drink   as-for
"Your drink?"
"What would you like to drink?" (PL3-4)

Izumi: はい。ビール を ください。
Hai.   Biiru   o   kudasai.
yes   beer   (obj.) please give
"(Yes), beer please." (PL3)

- the honorific *o-* in front of *nomimono* is optional, but a waiter would almost always use it with a customer.
- Izumi's *hai* does not really mean "yes," but simply indicates that she heard the waiter and is going to respond. See Basic Japanese No. 25.

© Hoshisato Mochiru / *Ribingu Gēmu,* Shogakukan

Tsukemono = "Pickles"

The woman in this scene is picking up a few things at the local vegetable stand, and as an afterthought decides she wants some Japanese pickles (*tsukemono*) as well. The word *tsukemono* is from the verb 漬ける *tsukeru* ("soak/pickle").

Customer: ここ の 漬け物 は おいしい わ ねぇ。
Koko no tsukemono wa oishii wa nē
here 's Japanese pickles as-for tasty (fem.)(colloq.)
"The *tsukemono* here sure are good, aren't they." (PL2-3)

Shopkeeper: ハハハ なんせ 良く 手入れしてる から ねぇ。
Ha ha ha nanse yoku te-ire shite-ru kara nē
(laugh) after all much/often are taking care of because (colloq.)
"Ha ha ha, after all, we take good care of them." (PL3)

• *tsukemono* is often translated as "pickle(s)," but that alone can be misleading. *Tsukemono* can be made from many different vegetables and pickling bases. The end result frequently bears little resemblance to what Westerners think of as a pickle.
• *nanse* is a colloquial variation of *nanishiro*, "anyhow/after all."
• one might think that the shopkeeper was making a play on words, since *te-ire suru* is written with the kanji for "hand" and "put in/enter," and she is sticking her hand in the barrel in this scene. The expression is entirely idiomatic, however, and *te-ire suru* retains none of its literal meaning. *Tsukemono* connoisseurs tell us that the *tsukemono* base requires frequent stirring and other maintenance, so good *tsukemono* require a lot of hard work.

Otoshimono = "Something dropped"

Many other verbs can be made into *mono* nouns. In this example, the verb is *otosu*, "drop," which becomes *otoshimono*, "(a) dropped object."

© Akizuki Risu / *OL Shinkaron*, Kodansha

Kachō: おい、落しもの
Oi, otoshimono
hey dropped object
"Hey, (it's a) dropped object."
"Hey, you dropped something." (PL2)

• his incomplete sentence suggests, "*. . . otoshimono (desu),*" "(. . . there's/it's a) dropped object." It is possible to phrase this sentence something like, "*nanika otoshita yo*" "(you) dropped something," but in Japanese it's probably more common to call attention to the dropped object the way he does here.
• *oi* is an abrupt way of getting someone's attention.

Namakemono = "Lazybones"

It's also possible to form nouns from verb stems combined with the *mono* that means "person," giving the meaning of "someone who is ～" In this scene, Kōsuke's landlady wants him to give her a hand in the garden.

Landlady: おーい、ナマケもん!!
Ōi, namakemon!!
hey lazy/idle person
"Hey, lazybones!" (PL2)

• *namakemon(o)* is from the verb *namakeru*, "be lazy/idle."

Tsukaimono ni naru = "Be something/someone useful"

Akagawa has pulled some strings to bring Ishii, a friend from his college days, on as a bellman at the first-class Hotel Platon. Ishii quit his job at a bank two years ago, and hasn't been able to hold down a regular job since. At the hotel, Ishii proves clumsy in both word and action, so the staff is beginning to understand why none of his other jobs went well.

© Ishinomori Shōtarō / *Hotel*, Shogakukan

Matsuda: あれじゃ　使いもの　に　ならん...!!
Are　ja　tsukaimono　ni　naran...!!
that　if it is　something useful　to　won't become
"Being like that, he isn't going to be anything of use!"
"Being like that, he's not going to work out!" (PL2)

Akagawa: わかってます...
Wakatte-masu
understand
"I know . . ." (PL3)

- the long dash before Matsuda's first word *are* indicates that this is the continuation of a sentence from the previous frame, where he was saying, "No matter how much of a friend he is ～"
- ～ *ja* is a colloquial contraction of ～ *de wa*, "if it is ～"
- *tsukaimono ni naran* is a contraction of *tsukaimono ni naranai*, a set phrase meaning, "is of no use/won't do." *Tsukaimono* ("something useful") is from the verb *tsukau* ("use").

Mono ni naru = "Amount to something/be somebody"

The example above, *tuskaimono ni naranai* "won't do/is of no use," leads us to this next phrase, *mono ni naru*, "amount to something/prove successful." The father in this scene owns a barber shop and is yelling at his eldest son for botching a practice haircut on the younger son. He uses the negative form, *mono ni naranai*, to mean "won't amount to anything."

Father: まったく　　　不器用な　奴　だ　な!!
Mattaku　　bukiyō na　yatsu da　na!!
utterly/completely　clumsy/unskillful　guy　is　(colloq.)

そんな　こと　じゃ　何年たっても、　ものにならねえ　ぞ。
Sonna　koto　ja　nan nen tatte mo,　mono ni naranē　zo.
that kind of　thing　if it is　however many years pass　amount to nothing　(emph.)
"You sure are a clumsy goof! At this rate, you'll never amount to anything no matter how many years go by." (PL2)

"Sound" FX: ガミ　ガミ
Gami gami　(effect of scolding someone)

© Saigan Ryōhei / *San-chōme no Yūhi*, Shogakukan

- *yatsu* is a slightly derogatory word for "person." It is often translated as "guy/fellow," but has a harsher feel than such a translation might suggest.
- *ja* is a contraction of *de wa*.
- *naranē* is a rough/masculine form of *naranai*, "won't become."
- *zo* is a rough/masculine particle which adds emphasis.

Sono mono = "Per se"

Sono mono, literally "that thing," is used to express the idea of "per se" or " . . . the very thing (itself)." This woman has been talking about a problem at work, and goes on with the discussion without realizing that her friend has wandered off to look at some clothes.

© Akizuki Risu / *OL Shinkaron*, Kōdansha

Woman: だから　　問題　は　　会社　の　システム そのもの
Dakara mondai wa kaisha no shisutemu sono mono
therefore problem as for company 's system itself

に ある　　わけ　　　よ　ね。つまり...
ni aru wake yo ne. Tsumari...
at exists situation/reason (emph.) (colloq.) that is
**"So (the situation is that) the problem is in the
company's system itself. In other words . . ."** (PL2)

Taishita mono = "Quite something"

The word *taishita* means "great/grand/important," and *taishita mono (da/desu)* indicates admiration, wonder, or amazement. The old woman in this scene has taken a ride with a man who accidently popped into her house in a time machine. After visiting prehistoric Japan and having a near miss with a dinosaur, she jumps 22 years ahead of her own time (1961) to 1983, and is amazed at all of the changes and progress.

Old Woman: ウヒョーッ テレビ に 色　が　ついとる わい!!
Uhyō! Terebi ni iro ga tsuitoru wai!!
wow TV to color (subj.) is attached (emph.)
"Wow! The television has color!" (PL2)

大したもん じゃ。
Taishita mon ja.
really something is
"That's really something!" (PL2)

• *tsuitoru* is a contraction of *tsuite-oru*, equivalent to *tsuite-
iru*. Older people frequently use *-oru* instead of *-iru*.
• other elements associated with the speech of older people
are *wai* instead of *wa* as a colloquial particle of emphasis,
and *ja* instead of *da* ("is/are").

© Saigan Ryōhei / *San-chōme no Yūhi*, Shogakukan

Monosugoi = "Tremendous/incredible"

Mono can be attached as a prefix to certain words to act as an intensifier. One of the most common of these "intensified" words is *monosugoi* ("tremendous/incredible"), from *sugoi* ("amazing/terrific"). In this scene, Yawara is in the middle of an intense judo bout. The winner will advance to the final, gold-medal match of the Barcelona Olympics, but so far, neither contestant has been able to get the upper hand.

© Urusawa Naoki / *Yawara!*, Shogakukan

Announcer: ものすごい 技 の 応酬!! ものすごい スピード!!
Monosugoi waza no ōshū!! Monosugoi supiido!!
incredible technique 's response incredible speed
"An intense exchange of blows! Such incredible speed!" (PL2)

Sound FX: ハァ ハァ ハァ ハァ
Hā hā hā hā
(sound of heavy breathing)

• *waza* refers to a technique or "move," and *waza no ōshū*, lit. "technique's response" indicates the moves and counter-moves that are going on in the match.

"Sound" FX: バッ
Ba! (effect of a sudden movement; quickly standing up in this case)

Monotarinai = "Something lacking"

Another example of *mono* as an intensifier is *monotarinai*, "not quite enough/have something lacking" from *tarinai*, "insufficient/lacking." Kōsuke had some old newspapers stacking up, so he decided to use them to clean the windows of his apartment building. He found the task somehow satisfying, and now he can't seem to stop.

Narration: アパート の 廊下 の ガラス だけ では もの足りない ので、
Apāto no rōka no garasu dake de wa monotarinai node,
apartment 's hall 's glass only with something lacking because

大家 の 家 の ガラス も みがき に 行った。
ōya no ie no garasu mo migaki ni itta.
landlord 's house 's glass also polish/clean to went
"Doing just the windows in the hallway of the apartment left me wanting to do more, so I went to do the landlady's windows as well." (PL2)

Sound FX: きゅっ きゅっ きゅっ きゅっ
Kyu! kyu! kyu! kyu!
(squeaking sound of polishing glass with newspaper)

• using a verb stem (here *migaki*, from *migaku*, "polish/wash") plus *ni iku/itta* means "go/went to do (the action)."

© Maekawa Tsukasa / *Dai-Tōkyō Binbō Seikatsu Manyuaru*, Kodansha

~ *mono ka* = "No way"

Strictly speaking, adding *mono ka* after a verb makes a question ("is it such a thing/situation that I would ~?"), but the phrase actually functions as a strong defiant assertion that one will not do the action in question. In this scene, the awards ceremony where judo star Yawara is to receive the National Medal of Honor has been thrown into disarray. She tries to make a quick exit with Matsuda, the young reporter she is secretly attracted to, but he gets clobbered by a mob of people who think he's a troublemaker out to disrupt the proceedings. This man, Kazamatsuri, has feelings for Yawara, and shouts at the downed Matsuda.

© Urusawa Naoki / *Yawara!*, Shogakukan

Kazamatsuri:
ざまをみろ!! そう 簡単に 柔さん を 渡す ものか!!
Zama o miro!! Sō kantan ni Yawara-san o watasu mono ka!!
serves you right that easily (name-hon.) (obj.) hand over no way
"See what you get? There's no way I'll give up Yawara that easily!" (PL2)

柔さん、 今 僕 が あなたの もと へ まいります!!
Yawara-san, ima boku ga anata no moto e mairimasu!!
(name-hon.) now I/me (subj.) your base/place to will go
"Yawara, now I'm coming to you!" (PL3-4)

- *zama o miro*, lit. "look at/see the predicament," is a phrase meaning "serves you right!/there!/see what you get?!"
- *anata no moto* is literally "your place/base," but means, "(the area/place) where you are."
- *mairimasu* is the PL3 form of *mairu*, a humble equivalent of *iku* ("go"), or *kuru* ("come"). In this case the Japanese equivalent is *iku* ("go") since he will be moving toward her, but the English is more natural as "come."

Mono o iu = "Carries weight/has effect"

Mono o iu literally means "~ says something," but it means "carries weight/has significance." Here, someone is trying to implicate foreign minister Sakaki in a scandal by exposing past relations he had with a female terrorist. His colleague Ogura takes it in stride.

Ogura: あったことはあった、 無かったことは無かった...
Atta koto wa atta, nakatta koto wa nakatta ...
what was, was what wasn't, wasn't

と いう 保身 に 走らぬ 毅然とした 態度
to iu hoshin ni hashiranu kizen to shita taido
(quote) called self-protection to doesn't run resolute attitude

が モノを言う!
ga mono o iu!
(subj.) says something.
"His resolute, non-defensive 'what happened happened and what didn't didn't' attitude says it all." (PL2)

- *hashiranu* is an equivalent of *hashiranai*, negative of *hashiru* "run." The negative made by using *-nu* where one would normally use *-nai* is an archaic form still in use in some expressions and phrases.
- 金がものを言う *Kane ga mono o iu* ("Money talks") is another interesting application of this idiom.

あったことはあった、無かったことは無かった...という保身に走らぬ毅然とした態度がモノを言う!

© Kawaguchi Kaji / *Medusa*, Shogakukan

MANGAJIN 's
BASIC JAPANESE through comics

Lesson 37 • Slang & Colloquialisms (1)

In this issue, we decided to present what is probably the most fun part of any language, and occasionally the most useful as well: slang. In our search for samples, however, we soon found ourselves in a muddle over the differences between slang, idioms, and colloquialisms. Hence we decided to expand our scope to include any type of "slangy" expression that you're likely to hear in the street but may have difficulty finding later on in your standard dictionary.

We can hardly attempt to cover the whole spectrum here, so we focused on what we felt were the more common slang words and idiomatic usages. We hope you enjoy them.

Mote-mote = "Be popular"

The women here have found out that Kameyama is capable of fathering healthy, energetic children, while the rest of the (better looking) men can sire only dull, listless kids.

© Okazaki Jirō / *After Zero*, Shogakukan

Narration:

今や　　彼は　他の　　誰　　よりも
imaya　kare wa　hoka no　dare　yori mo
now-(emph)　he　as for　other　who/someone　more than

モテモテの　人生　を　楽しんでいる　　の　だった。
mote-mote no jinsei o tanoshinde-iru no datta.
popular　　　life　(obj.)　is enjoying　(explan.)　was
"Now he was enjoying a life of popularity more than anyone else."
"All of a sudden, he was enjoying more popularity than anyone else." (PL2)

Kameyama:

じゃ、お先に。
Ja,　　o-saki ni
well　(hon.)-before
"Well, (I'll take my leave) before you."
"Bye, guys." (PL2)

* *imaya*, used mainly in written language, is an emphatic form of *ima* in which "now" has the sense of "as opposed to before." The idea is that Kameyama's popularity is newfound.
* *o-saki ni* is short for *o-saki ni shitsurei shimasu*, lit. "I'm being rude by leaving before you." It is a standard way to say good-bye when leaving before others. Here he is being a bit flip.

> *Mote-mote* is from the verb *moteru*, "be popular (with the opposite sex)," which itself borders on slang. *Mote-mote* is used for being popular in this sense, and sometimes in a more general sense as well—for example, to refer to entertainers who are hot.

Ikasu = "Sharp"

This man is showing off his new set of clothes to a buddy.

> **Man:** どうだ。 / いかす だろ。
> *Dō da.* / *Ikasu daro.*
> how is it   cool/sharp right?
> **"What do you think? Pretty sharp, huh?"** (PL3)

Ikasu = "(be) sharp/smart/cool." It is primarily used by men, while *suteki* would be more commonly used by women. The literal meaning of *ikasu* is "cause to go," so the feeling is something like, "it really sends me." A related *iku* colloquialism is *ikeru* (lit. "can go"), which means "(be) quite good/delicious," as in *kono sake wa ikeru.* The word *ikasu* has been in use for many years.

© Ueda Masashi / *Furiten-kun,* Take Shobo

Dasai = "Hick"

This man has just informed his girlfriend that his family are farmers, and if they get married, they will work the farm together.

© Deluxe Company / *Zusetsu Gendai Yōgo Binran,* Futabasha

> **Man:** あっ、まって!
> *A!*   *Matte!*
> **"Hey, wait!"** (PL2)
>
> **Woman:** ダサーイ,サイテー
> *Dasa-i,*   *saitē*
> hick-ish   lowest
> **"What a rube! That's the pits!"** (PL2)

- she elongates the word *dasai* to *dasa-i* for emphasis.
- *Saitē* is a pop spelling of *saitei* (最低), lit. "the lowest."

Dasai is a slang word for something countrified, hick-ish, or just generally uncool. According to 現代用語の基礎知識 (*Gendai Yōgo no Kiso Chishiki,* "Essential Knowledge of Current Terms"), it seems to come from the word 田舎 ("country/rural area"), normally read *inaka* but in this case corrupted to *dasha* (based on alternate readings of the same kanji). The adjective form, *dashai,* became *dasai.*

Busu = "Ugly"

Reiko has always had (unwarranted) confidence in her appearance, but at a recent *o-miai* meeting for an arranged marriage, the man she was considering made a negative comment about her looks.

Busu is a very common slang word for referring to an ugly woman. As such, it is similar to the western slang word "dog." There are several theories as to the origin of the word. *Bu* (無, 不) added to a noun makes it negative (like adding "un-" or "dis-"). By extension, *bu* can have the implication of "bad" → "ugly." Another theory is that *busu* is from the Ainu word *pushu,* meaning "ugly," and yet another is that *busu* is from the name of a lethal poison that causes the ingester's face to contort hideously.

> **Reiko:** あたしって ブス?
> *Atashi* *tte*   *busu?*
> I/me as-for ugly
> **"You think I'm a dog?"** (PL2)

- *tte* here stands for *to iu no wa* and functions like the topic marker *wa.*

© Kubonouchi Eisaku / *Tsurumoku Dokushin Ryō,* Shogakukan

Dekai = "Big"

A visitor from Japan has just arrived in New York and taken a taxi. He has apparently been in the States before.

© Kawaguchi Kaiji / *Chinmoku no Kantai*, Kodansha

Visitor: いつ来ても　アメリカ はでかい 国 だ。
Itsu kite mo　Amerika wa dekai kuni da.
whenever (I) come America as-for huge country is
"Whenever I come, America is a huge country."
"Every time I come, I'm impressed by what a huge country America is." (PL2)

これほど 文化 も 人種 も ゴッタ煮で。
Kore hodo bunka mo jinshu mo gotta-ni de.
this much culture also races also melting pot is
"Such a melting pot of cultures and races . . ." (PL2)

- the second sentence is not complete. It could be an afterthought, or simply an unfinished sentence.

> *Dekai* (or sometimes *dekkai*) is a slang word for "big" that has been in use since well before the modern era. While it is generally considered a not very ladylike term, some women, particularly in the country, use it freely even in polite conversation. It may come from *do* (an intensifying prefix) or *dai* (大) + *ikai* (厳い, basically a synonym for *ōkii*, "large/great/massive").
>
> *Gotta* comes from the "mimetic" FX word *gota-gota*, representing items in congested confusion. *Ni* (煮) is from the verb *niru* ("boil"), so *gotta-ni* is "things thrown together in no order and boiled" → "stew/melting pot."

Naui = "Now-ish"

This OL has just told her friends, who are on their way to the golf course, that she is going cycling. They reply that cycling is *jimi*, "plain/quiet/sober."

OL: これ だから ミーハー は　　いや　よ。
Kore dakara miihā wa iya yo.
this because airheads as for disagreeable (emph.)
サイクリング って ナウイ の よっ。
Saikuringu tte naui no yo!
cycling as for with it (explan.) (emph.)
"That's why I hate airheads. Cycling is what's really 'in' now, you know." (PL2)

- *iya* means "distasteful/disagreeable." (See Basic Japanese No. 33). *Yo* often takes the place of *da/desu yo*, especially in feminine speech.
- *tte* here stands for *to iu no wa* and functions like the topic marker *wa*.

© Akizuki Risu / *OL Shinkaron*, Kodansha

> *Miihā* is a derogatory term aimed at people, usually young women, who are bubble-headed, frivolous and generally sheep-like in their behavior—*e.g.*, those who run in a pack screaming after pop stars. It is thought to come from the beginning sounds of the diminutive forms (*Mii-chan* and *Hā-chan*) of common female names.
>
> *Naui* ("trendy/in") is taken from the English word "now." One would normally expect the form *nau na* for an imported adjective, but in this case it became "trendy" to turn it into an *i*-adjective. In recent times, *naui* as a word has gone the way of most other *naui* things and become somewhat passé.

Sekoi = "Petty/Self-serving"

Ōhashi, who is hoping to improve business at his *yakitori* restaurant, has decided to spend a night at the Hotel Platon to observe how they treat their customers. When Matsuda offers to give him some help, the other employees jokingly accuse him of trying to ingratiate himself to get a free meal or two at the *yakitori* restaurant.

© Ishinomori Shōtarō / *Hotel*, Shogakukan

Matsuda: バ・バカモン!! / 私 は
Ba, bakamon!! / Watashi wa
Ri-ridiculous   I/me as for

そんな セコイ 人間 ではな～～い!!
sonna sekoi ningen de wa na–i!!
that kind of petty human am not
"(Don't be) absurd! I'm not such a chintzy person!" (PL2)

Ōhashi: ハハハ
Ha ha ha
"Ha ha ha"

> *Sekoi* is a slang word covering a range of meanings, including "chintzy," "petty," "small-minded," "mean," "nitpicky," and "self-serving."

Toraburu = "Be troubled"

Inokuma Yawara has gone looking for Hanazono at the judo dojo where he practices, but the members tell her that he is off somewhere else.

Boy 1: いえね、 なんか 最近 女性 問題 で
ie ne, nanka saikin josei mondai de
you see, something lately girl/woman problem with

トラブってる らしい ん です よ。
torabutte-ru rashii n desu yo.
is troubled it seems (explan.) is (emph.)
"Well, you see, it seems that he's been troubled over some girl lately." (PL2)

© Urusawa Naoki / *Yawara!*, Shogakukan

Boy 2: 猪熊さん も 気をつけた ほうがいい です よ。
Inokuma-san mo ki o tsuketa hō ga ii desu yo.
(name -hon) also is/was/be careful is better to is (emph.)
"Ms. Inokuma should be careful, too."
"You should be careful, too, Inokuma." (PL2)

• Japanese speakers often use the listener's name where an English speaker would say "you."

> *Toraburu,* taken from the English word "trouble," is used both as a noun ("trouble") and, more recently, as a verb ("be troubled/trouble over"). Its use as a verb is based in the fact that it ends in *ru,* and thus can be conjugated like any other *ru* verb, as shown in the example above. *Daburu* ("to double/be doubled/be layered"), from the English word "double," works the same way. In written Japanese, this type of word is written entirely in katakana (トラブル) when used as a noun, but gets a hiragana *ru* (トラブる) when used as a verb.

Etchi = "Lewd"

Kōsaku is talking to himself about some business he wants to take care of, but his co-worker Kuniko, who has been chasing him for some time, thinks he is referring to something else . . .

Kōsaku: 今晩　こそ　一発　きめて...
Konban koso ippatsu kimete . . .
tonight indeed one shot determine
"Tonight for sure, I'm going to decide it in one shot."
<u>**"Tonight for sure, I'm just gonna do it!"**</u> (PL2)

Kuniko: やだあ、エッチィ！耕作 ったら!!
Ya da–, etchi! Kōsaku ttara!!
distasteful lewd/indecent (name) (quote)
<u>**"Ew, how lewd! Kōsaku!"**</u> (PL2)

© Urusawa Naoki / *Yawara!*, Shogakukan

- *ippatsu*, lit. "a single burst," can be used to indicate a variety of things that "go off" with a shot, such as gunshots, punches, etc. In this case, Kuniko mistakenly thinks that Kōsaku is using it to refer to a sexual encounter.
- *ya da–* is a colloquial form of *iya da,* used to express disgust/dislike (genuine or feigned) for something. See Basic Japanese No. 33.
- *ttara* is a contraction of *to ittara,* a conditional "if/when" form of *to iu* ("say ～"), so it literally means "if I speak of ～" In colloquial speech, *ttara* is sometimes used in place of *wa* to mark the topic, usually with a feeling of disapproval/beratement.

> *Etchi* (エッチ) is another well-used slang word. It is thought to be a Japanese pronunciation of the letter H, which most references agree stands for the Japanese word *hentai* ("abnormality/perversion"). *Etchi* does not actually refer to the abnormal or perverted, however; it simply means "indecent/lewd/dirty." Like the word *sukebei/sukebe* ("lewd/lecherous"), it is often used as a verbal reprimand to someone who has done, said, or implied something lewd. The *Shogakukan Nihon Kokugo Daijiten* tells us that *eichi* (エイチ), a slightly different pronunciation for the letter H, is used among female students as slang for "husband," so correct pronunciation here is crucial.

Dekite-iru = "Having a relationship"

Shōta's friend was expecting him to invite Miyuki along on a ski trip they were planning, as the two seemed to be a couple. Shōta, however, denies any such relationship.

Shōta: ち、違う　よ! オレは...
Chi, chigau yo! Ore wa . . .
different/incorrect (emph.) I/me as for
<u>**"Y, you've got it wrong! I . . ."**</u> (PL2)

Friend: オレ は てっきり、正太 と みゆきさん
Ore wa tekkiri, Shōta to Miyuki-san
I/me as for beyond doubt (name) and (name -hon)

デキてる　もん と 思ってた ん やけど な!
dekite-ru mon to omotte-ta n ya kedo na!
having a relationship thing (quote) was thinking (explan.) but (colloq.)
<u>**"I was dead sure that you and Miyuki were an item."**</u> (PL2)

© Kubonouchi Eisaku / *Tsuramoku Dokushin Ryō*, Shogakukan

- *tekkiri* is a slangy word meaning "completely/beyond all doubt."
- *dekite-ru* is a contraction of *dekite-iru*.
- *mon* is short for *mono*, lit. "thing" but in this case more abstractly meaning "situation/circumstance." See Basic Japanese Nos. 35 & 36.
- *ya kedo* is a dialect version of *da kedo*, lit. "but." Some form of "but" is often tacked onto the end of a sentence to "soften" it.

> The slang word *dekite-iru* strongly connotes physical intimacy, but can be used to mean simply "going steady/involved in a relationship."

Nanpa suru = "Hit on"

Looking out the lodge window, Shōta and Nao-chan spot three young men pestering Miyuki as she tries to ski.

© Kubonouchi Eisaku / *Tsurumoku Dokushin Ryō*, Shogakukan

Nanpa suru (軟派する) is the expression for "hitting on" or "trying to pick up." The first kanji means "soft," and the second is "group/faction/school." It is used in contrast to 硬派 (*kōha*), the "hard school," which refers to the tough, macho type who must pretend not to be interested in things like girls. The passive form, *nanpa sareru,* is used for "to be hit on."

Nao-chan:

地元 で スキー の インスト やってる 連中 よ!
Jimoto de sukii no insuto yatte-ru renchū yo!
local at ski of instruction are doing guys/group (emph.)

ナンパ ばっか して さぁ、ガラ悪い ん だ よ!
Nanpa bakka shite sā, gara warui n da yo!
hitting on only do (colloq.) ill-bred (explan.) is (emph.)
"Those are the local guys who work here as ski instructors! They don't do anything but hit on girls, you know. How crass." (PL2)

あたしも 声かけられた もん!
Atashi mo koe kakerareta mon!
I/me also was talked to (explan.)
"They approached me, too." (PL2)

- *yatte-ru* is a contraction of *yatte-iru* "are doing."
- *bakka* is a colloquial contraction of *bakari,* "only/nothing but."
- *gara warui,* lit. "(a) bad pattern/design," means "ill-bred/vulgar."
- *koe (o) kakeru,* is the past passive form of *koe (o) kakeru,* literally "put (a) voice on." This is the standard way to say that you approached someone verbally, or in the passive case, were approached verbally by someone.

Suppokasu = "Stand (someone) up"

Teruko is a bit forceful by nature. To thank Yamaoka for keeping her company while she was waiting for someone a few nights ago, she invites him for dinner at a restaurant. Of course, her way of inviting him is to tell him that he <u>will</u> be there.

Teruko: 七時 よ! わかった わね!
Shichi-ji yo! Wakatta wa ne!
7 o'clock (emph.) understood (fem. colloq.)
"Seven o'clock! You got it?!" (PL2)

すっぽかしたりしたら タダじゃ おかない わ よ!
Suppokashitari shitara tada ja okanai wa yo!
if do something like stand up with nothing won't let be (fem.) (emph.)
"Don't you go standing me up or you'll never hear the end of it!" (PL2)

- *suppokashitari shitara* is from *suppokasu.* Using the *-tari* form of a verb (usually followed by some form of *suru,* in this case *shitara*) means, "do something like ～"
- *tada ja okanai* means "won't let it go easily/it won't end without trouble."

© Kariya & Hanasaki / *Oishinbo*, Shogakukan

Suppokasu is slang for "stand someone up/break a promise" or "leave work undone." *Su!* (すっ) is a prefix for emphasis, and *hokasu* (ほかす) means "cast down/cast aside/abandon." (The *h* changes to *p* for euphony.) Note that *hokasu* on its own is no longer used in standard Japanese, though it does continue to be used in Kansai dialect.

BASIC JAPANESE through comics

Lesson 38 • Slang & Colloquialisms (2)

Did you ever wonder how to call someone a "klutz" in Japanese? Well, you're about to find out. Last issue, we kicked off the series on slang and colloquialisms, featuring some of the more widely used terms. In this second, final installment, we continue with that approach, presenting common colloquialisms and throwing in an insulting term or two for fun.

   While there are slang dictionaries and guidebooks, these tend to focus on outrageous or inflammatory expressions and to overlook the basic, everyday slang. Our goal is to present you with a taste of what you might hear in normal, casual Japanese conversations, or, at the least, on Japanese television.

Kokeru = "Fall down"

The gang from the Tsurumoku company dorm for single employees has gone on a skiing trip. Most of them have skiied before, but Miyuki is a rank beginner.

© Kubonouchi Eisaku / *Tsurumoku Dokushin Ryō,* Shogakukan

Miyuki: あ〜〜ん!
Ā–n!
(voiced sigh of disappointment)

また コケちゃった!!
mata   kokechatta!!
again   fell down (-regret)
"Ooohhh, I fell down again!" (PL2)

• *kokechatta* is a colloquial contraction of *kokete shimatta,* the plain past form of *kokete shimau,* from *kokeru* (see below). The *-te shimau* form implies that the action or result is regrettable/undesirable (or sudden/complete). See Basic Japanese No. 44.

Kokeru means "trip" or "fall down" (*korobu* or *korogaru* in standard Japanese). *Kokeru* has a long history of usage, and while not really slang, it is considered highly colloquial. Other meanings, depending on context, of course, include "fail/flop," "get arrested," and "go bankrupt."

Kiseru = "Pull a train-pass scam"

It looks like the conductor is coming to check the passengers' tickets, and Furiten has cause
for concern . . .

© Ueda Masashi / *Furiten-kun*, Take Shobō

Furiten: やべ　　　　　　やべ。
Yabe　　　　　　　*yabe.*
dangerous/awkward　dangerous/awkward

オレ　　キセル　　なん　だ　よ　ね。
Ore　　*kiseru*　　*nan*　*da*　*yo*　*ne.*
I/me　ride w/o proper ticket (explan.) is (emph.) (colloq.)
"Uh-oh, this is bad. I'm pulling a *kiseru*."
(PL2)

- *yabe* is a "rougher" version of *yabai,* a slang word that
  means "dangerous/awkward" in the sense that trouble is
  on the horizon. *Yabai* comes from *yaba,* a noun meaning
  "danger/trouble" that is not used in modern Japanese.

Regular commuters in Japan usually buy train passes good for un-
limited rides between two points for a specified period of time. The
machine or person checking passes at the exit gate has no way of
knowing when passengers originally boarded, allowing for all sorts
of illicit riding activity. One way dishonest commuters abuse the
system is by purchasing two passes, each good for only a short section at either end of the commute, and then riding the middle part for
free. Taking advantage of this and similar tricks to get a free ride is
called *kiseru-nori* ("*kiseru*-riding"). The word comes from a tobacco
pipe comprised of a metal mouthpiece and bowl connected by a long
bamboo pipe. Because a *kiseru* pipe has metal (*kane,* symbolizing
gold/money) only at the two ends, it is likened to the practice of paying for tickets/passes at either end of a commute and riding free for
the longer middle portion. *Kiseru-nori* is illegal, of course, but widely
practiced (forcing conductors to occasionally check tickets/passes on
the train, as Furiten thinks is happening in the example above).

Nekobaba = "Pocket (something)/Embezzle"

This man was bowing down as the local magistrate passed by, and while kneeling he
spotted a coin—which the magistrate has presumably dropped.

Man: とどけよう　　か　ネコババ　しよ　か...
Todokeyō　　*ka*　*nekobaba*　*shiyo*　*ka*...
shall report/deliver (?) pocket/swipe shall do (?)

とどけよう　　か　ネコババ　しよ　か...
Todokeyō　　*ka*　*nekobaba*　*shiyo*　*ka*...
shall report/deliver (?) pocket/swipe shall do (?)
"Should I turn it in, or should I pocket it . . .
Should I turn it in, or pocket it?" (PL2)

- *todokeyō* is the "will/shall" form of *todokeru,* "report/send,"
  and *shiyo* is a shortened *shiyō,* the "will/shall" form of *suru*
  ("do"). This repeated *-yō ka* pattern (e.g. *todokeyō ka
  nekobaba shiyō ka*) is used when one is torn or trying to
  decide between two alternative actions.

© Ueda Masashi / *Furiten-kun*, Take Shobō

Nekobaba means "cat excrement," and adding a form of *suru*
makes it a verb. The implication here is that cats quickly cover
their mess and hide it when done. An alternate theory of the term's
derivation links it to an old lady in the mid-Tokugawa era who
loved cats but was very greedy (*neko* is "cat" and *baba/babā* is a
somewhat derogatory word for "old woman"). The slang term
can mean: 1) hide a misdeed; 2) embezzle; 3) keep something as
one's own instead of trying to return it to the rightful owner. This
particular case is an example of #3.

Hoshi = "Perp/Suspect"

The police are looking over a crime scene for clues.

© Aoki Kimuko / *Gokigen Ne, Dadii*, Scholar Publishers

Policeman: ガイ者 は ここ で ホシ に 撃たれて。
Gaisha wa koko de hoshi ni utarete.
victim as for here at suspect/perp by was shot-and
"The victim was shot by the perp here..." (PL2)

- *gaisha* is police slang for "victim." It's simply a short form of *higaisha* (被害者, "victim/injured party").
- *utarete* is the continuing form of *utareru,* which is the passive of *utsu,* "shoot." The continuing form implies that there is more to the expressed thought.

> *Hoshi* is a police slang word for a suspect or perpetrator of a crime. As such, it is similar to the English slang word "perp."
> *Hoshi* can be written with the kanji for "star/planet" (星). The slang usage is apparently related to words such as *zuboshi* (図星, "bull's-eye/mark"), and *meboshi* (目星, "aim/objective" → "person singled out as a suspect").

Deka = "Police detective"

A police detective has just searched this *yakuza* kingpin's office for morphine, but turned up nothing illegal. When the gangster haughtily asked him what he found, the detective lost his temper and pounded his fist on the desk.

Yakuza boss: 怖い 刑事(でか)さん だ な
Kowai deka-san da na.
scary/frightening police detective -(hon.) is (colloq.)
"That's one scary cop." (PL2)

© Okazaki Jirō / *After Zero*, Shogakukan

- in Japanese, a writer has the option of specifying or clarifying the reading of kanji by "spelling it out" phonetically in hiragana or katakana beside the kanji. (These readings are called *furigana*.) Alternate readings are often given for "standard" kanji when someone is using slang or contractions in manga. The kanji 刑事 are read *keiji,* which is the conventional term for a "police detective." *Deka,* the reading provided in *furigana,* indicates what the speaker actually said. For a more in-depth look at such creative kanji readings, see Basic Japanese No. 7.

> *Deka* is slang for police detective. In the Meiji era, detectives wore *kakusode* (a traditional type of Japanese garment) instead of police uniforms, making them "plainclothes" policemen in a sense. The word *deka* represents the first and last sounds of *kakusode* in reverse. (Reversing the syllables/sounds of a word to create slang terms is a common practice.) The word started out as slang among outlaws, and then entered into general use. *Deka* is not an offensive term, and is used among the police themselves, much like the word "cop" in English.

Gūtara = "Goof-off"

Section chief Iigura hates squid and refuses to allow the company store to sell it simply for this reason. Yamaoka, a connoisseur of fine food, feels that Iigura has probably never had "good" squid, and that is why he can't stand it. Now Yamaoka has wagered that he can make squid that Iigura will actually like. If Yamaoka loses the bet, he must quit his job, and Iigura was never fond of him in the first place . . .

© Kariya & Hanasaki / *Oishinbo*, Shogakukan

Iigura: これ で お前 という グータラ社員 を 厄介払い出来る わ!
Kore de omae to iu gūtara shain o yakkaibarai dekiru wa!
this with you called lazy employee (obj.) can get rid of (emph.)
"With this, I can get rid of the lazy employee called you."
"Now I can finally be rid of you, you good-for-nothing goof-off!"
(PL2)

- *wa* is a colloquial particle for emphasis that's typically feminine, but men can use it, with a slightly different inflection, without sounding effeminate.
- *yakkaibarai* implies getting rid of a nuisance.

> *Gūtara* is slang for "lazy/goof-off." It is often used in combination with nouns. For example, *Gūtara Mama* ("Lazy Mom") is a manga series by Furuya Mitsutoshi appearing in the *Mainichi Shinbun* Sunday edition. As a prefix, *gu* conveys a feeling of "foolish," and is used in such words as *gusai*. *Gusai* literally means "no-good/foolish wife," but is actually just a humble way of referring to one's own wife. *Gūtara* dates back to the pre-modern era.

Doji na = "Klutzy"

Mayumi is the first telepath on the moon. When she hears a voice in her head, she unthinkingly opens her helmet.

Mayumi:
なん て ドジな 話!! 全く ありえないこと!!
nan te doji na hanashi!! Mattaku arienai koto!!
what (quote) boneheaded story completely impossible thing
"What a stupid tale! It's completely impossible!"
"What a stupid thing to do! Can you believe it?" (PL2)

私 は 月面 で ヘルメット を 開けてしまった。
Watashi wa getsumen de herumetto o akete shimatta.
I/me (as for) moon surface at/on helmet (obj.) opened (-regret)
"I opened my helmet on the moon!" (PL2)

- *nan te* is a colloquial quotative form, short for *nan to iu,* which implies that the situation is surprising/hard to believe.

© Okazaki Jirō / *After Zero*, Shogakukan

> *Doji* by itself is a noun, meaning either "a bungler/klutz" or the "mistake/screw-up" such a person commits. *Doji na* is the adjective form, "boneheaded/stupid/klutzy." A common idiomatic form is *doji o fumu,* meaning "make a mess of things/bungle." Colloquially, it is also used in a verb form, *dojiru. Doji* may have origins in the word *donchi,* "dull," or possibly *tochiru,* "blow one's lines" or "screw up/bungle." Another explanation is that it is an abbreviation of *dojiguji,* "not make sense/not clear." The use of *doji* dates back to pre-modern times.

Kamo = "Sucker/Easy mark"

In a game of mahjongg, this man graciously offered to lend some money to another player who was running short. Little did the borrower know that the lender works for a loan company, and that there will be heavy interest to pay.

<u>**Agent:**</u> カモ 一人 つかまえた ぞー。
Kamo hitori tsukamaeta zo–.
dupe one person caught (emph.)
"I snared a pigeon." (PL2)

<u>**Boss:**</u> ごくろうさん。
Gokurō-san
hard worker
"Good work." (PL2)

<u>**On door:**</u> サラリー ローン
Sararii Rōn
Salary(man) Loan(s)

- *gokuro-san* is a way of thanking someone for his or her efforts. See Basic Japanese No. 20.

© Ueda Masashi / *Furiten-kun,* Take Shobō

> *Kamo* means "duck," so its slang use is very similar to that of "pigeon" in English to mean "sucker/dupe." It's used in expressions such as *Ii kamo ga negi o shotte kita,* literally, "A good duck has come bearing green onions," deriving from the practice of cooking duck with onions. The implication is, of course, that a prime sucker has appeared, ready to be cooked up and served for dinner.

Hira = "Peon/Grunt"

Hamasaki Densuke has never been very ambitious at work, content to stay at the same level indefinitely. He is discussing his current working conditions with his wife, and she asks if he doesn't at least have some rival whom he would like to outperform. He says no.

© Yamasaki & Kitami / *Tsuri Baka Nisshi,* Shogakukan

<u>**Wife:**</u> だから いつまでも ヒラ で
Dakara itsu made mo hira de
therefore forever low-level employee with/at

平気 なの よ ね。
heiki na no yo ne.
indifferent (explan.) (emph.) (colloq.)
"That's why you're satisfied to be an eternal grunt." (PL2)

<u>**Sound FX:**</u> ドタッ
Dota!
Thud! (slapstick effect of hitting the floor)

- *itsu made mo* is literally "until whenever," and means "forever/eternally/indefinitely."

> *Hira* (sometimes written with the kanji 平 which means "level/flat") usually refers to *hira-shain,* "rank-and-file employee," but it can refer to "ordinary/common" members of any organization, i.e. those without any managerial or leadership responsibilities. This ties in with the regular meaning of *hira,* "average/ordinary/non-special." *Hira* is more colloquial than slang.

Mabui = "Beautiful"

Mamoru-kun's little girlfriend had to move away when her father was transferred to a different city. He goes unannounced to see her and finds her walking with another boy. To save face, he tells her that he has a new girlfriend.

© Kubonouchi Eisaku / *Tsurumoku Dokushin Ryō*, Shogakukan

Mamoru-kun:

容姿　　　　バツグン!　スタイル　最高!
Yōshi　　*batsugun!*　*Sutairu*　*saikō!*
face & figure outstanding　　style ultimate/best
"A real looker. Totally stylish." (PL2)

ケチのつけようのない　マブイ　　女　　さ!!
Kechi no tsukeyō no nai　*mabui*　*onna*　*sa!!*
can't find fault with　　　beautiful girl/woman (emph.)
"A beauty of a girl with whom no one could find any fault!" (PL2)

- *yōshi* refers to a person's appearance, specifically the face and figure.
- *sutairu* is from the English "style."

> *Mabui* is slang for "beautiful/stunning." It seems to have come from the word *mabu,* which allegedly originated as underworld slang for "superior/good/beautiful (thing)," or for something that "goes splendidly/without a hitch." *Mabui* (眩い) is related to the word *mabushii* (眩しい, "bright/blinding"), but apparently was not directly derived from it. Although it appears in pre-modern Japanese literature, *mabui* today is used only in this slang/colloquial sense and is not considered "standard" Japanese.

Maji = "Serious"

Tadokoro is a police detective, and he has been talking with Q (who appears as a private eye in this story) about a man they're searching for. When Noriko sees a picture of the man, she pipes in that she has seen him recently.

© Tomisawa Chinatsu / *Katsushika Q*, Shogakukan

Tadokoro:　えっ、見た? マジ!?
　　　　　　　E! Mita? Maji!?
　　　　　　　huh saw serious
　　　　　　　"What? You saw him? Really?" (PL2)

Noriko:　うん。
　　　　　　Un.
　　　　　　"Uh-huh." (PL2)

- *un* shows agreement or is an informal "yes."

> *Maji* means "really/honestly/seriously." It is taken from the word *majime,* "serious/earnest." But while *majime* is often used to describe people who take work, life, etc., seriously, *maji* has more of a feeling of "no joke/honest."

BASIC JAPANESE through comics

Lesson 39 • The Many Faces of "Face" (1)

Our original intention in this lesson was to illustrate expressions related to "saving face" and "losing face," since these are such important concepts in Japanese society. But when we started looking at manga examples and found "face" appearing in all sorts of idiomatic expressions, we decided to broaden our scope and expand the lesson into two parts. The first part gives a sampling of general idiomatic expressions relating to "face," while the second delves into the cultural concept of face as "prestige" or "dignity."

Japanese has several words for "face." *Kao* (顔) is the generic word, while *tsura* (ツラ or 面) is a slang term with a slightly insulting air to it. *Men* (面) refers to a face or facet of something, and can sometimes be used to refer to a person's face as well. Some of the idiomatic and colloquial expressions appearing in this first part have surprisingly literal counterparts in English, while others are uniquely Japanese.

With all of these facial aspects thoroughly mastered, you should be able to face your Japanese friends with less fear of, well, losing face.

A good (looking) face

Arale, android creation of the brilliant but klutzy inventor Dr. Slump, has just discovered another piece of his handiwork. It seems that he has invented a camera which can take pictures of the future. He gives a quick demonstration, and Arale is duly impressed.

<u>Arale:</u> はかせ　　ってアタマいい　ん　だ　ね!
Hakase   tte atama ii   n   da ne!
professor/doctor (as for) head   good (explan.) is (colloq.)
"The Professor's head is good, isn't it."
"You're really smart, aren't you." (PL2)

<u>Dr. Slump:</u> ふふ...カオも　いい　けど　な。
Fu fu . . . Kao mo   ii   kedo na.
(laugh)   face also good   but (colloq.)
"Heh heh, my face is also good, though . . ."
"Heh heh. And handsome, too." (PL2)

- the title *hakase* generally refers to someone with a doctoral degree and may be translated as "Doctor" or "Professor."
- *kedo* literally means "but." Some form of "but" is often added to the end of a sentence to "soften" it.
- although her name, アラレ, would normally be romanized as *Arare*, the author of this manga prefers the spelling "Arale."

© Toriyama Akira / *Dr. Slump*, Shueisha

"Nice face" → Smile

Whereas *kao (mo/ga) ii* means "a good looking face," *ii kao* means "nice/smiling face." Kuniko, a photographer for a sports paper, is covering high school judo star Yawara's graduation. Yawara and Kuniko have had their differences, so Yawara is having trouble looking pleasant.

Kuniko: ハーイ、柔ちゃん！ いい 顔 ちょーだい!!
Ha-i,   Yawara-chan!   Ii kao   chōdai!
OK   (name-dim.)   good face   please
"OK Yawara, a good face please!"
"OK, Yawara, give me a nice smile now!" (PL2)

へんな 顔 が 記事に なっちゃう わよーー！
Hen na kao   ga   kiji ni   natchau   wa   yo–!
strange face (subj.) article to become-(regret) (fem.) (emph.)
"(Otherwise) that funny face will go into the article." (PL2)

Sound FX: タタッ
Ta ta!
(sound of quick footsteps as Kuniko approaches Yawara)

- *chōdai* is a colloquial way to say "please."
- *natchau* is a colloquial contraction of *natte shimau*. The *-te shimau* form implies that the action or result is regrettable/undesirable or complete/final. See Basic Japanese No. 44.

© Urusawa Naoki / *Yawara!*, Shogakukan

Frown on

Literally translated, *ii kao o shinai* means "not make a good face"; the actual meaning is similar to "frown upon/disapprove" in English. Kuwata works for a shady loan company, and is dealing with a potential borrower who already has several outstanding loans from other sources. Kuwata's boss agrees to grant the man a loan if they can get Masako, the man's daughter (who has a respectable job at the ward office) to cosign. Note that Kuwata speaks in strong Osaka dialect, so *ii kao shinai* becomes *ē kao sen*.

Kuwata: そんなら こう しよう。身内 は
Sonnara   kō   shiyō.   Miuchi wa
in that case this way let's do family as for

審査   が ええ顔せん の やけど、
shinsa   ga   ē kao sen   no   ya kedo,
credit examiners (subj.) frown on (explan.) but

正子 を 保証人 に 付けましょ。
Masako o   hoshōnin ni   tsukemasho.
(name) (obj.) guarantor as let's attach

"In that case, let's do it this way. The credit examiners frown on having family members (cosign), but let's put down Masako as a cosigner." (PL3-Kansai dialect)

- *sonnara* is a colloquial contraction of *sore nara,* "in that case."
- *ya kedo* is a dialect equivalent of *da kedo,* "but."

© Aoki Yūji / *Naniwa Kin'yudo*, Kodansha

"Do" a disagreeable face

In Japanese, you don't "make" or "pull" a face—you "do" (*suru*) one. This can be a bit confusing, since the same type of expression is used to mean that someone *has* a (round/shriveled/dopey, etc.) face, but the context will usually keep things clear. In this scene, Haguregumo is going out drinking with a few of his friends, and this old man asks if he can come along, too.

Old Man: あら、一瞬　いやな　顔　を　した　ね。
Ara,　isshun　iya na　kao　o　shita　ne.
oh my　an instant　disagreeable　face　(obj.)　did　(colloq.)

　いや　　　なの?
Iya　　　na no?
disagreeable　is it?

"Oh, my. For an instant you did a disagreeable face. Is it disagreeable?
"Uh-oh, for a second there you made a face. You don't want me along?" (PL2)

• *ara* is an interjection showing a sudden realization/awareness: "oh!/oh my!"
• *iya na* is an adjective meaning "unpleasant/disagreeable." See Basic Japanese No. 33 for a full treatment of *iya*.

© Akiyama Jōji / *Haguregumo*, Shogakukan

"Do" a difficult face

Shima has just found out that he is being transferred from Kyoto back to the main office in Tokyo. Now he has to tell Katsuko, whom he has grown rather fond of.

Katsuko: 何　を　そんなに　難しい　顔　してはる
Nani　o　sonna ni　muzukashii　kao　shite-haru
what　(obj.)　that much　difficult　face　do (-hon.)

ん　です　か、島さん。
n　desu　ka,　Shima-san.
(explan.)　is　(?)　(name-hon.)
"What are you looking so grim about, Shima-san?" (PL3)

• *muzukashii kao shite-haru* is an honorific dialect form of *muzukashii kao (o) shite-iru,* lit. "is/are doing/making a difficult face." The meaning of *muzukashii kao (o) shite-iru* is "have a grim/troubled expression." Using *-te haru* as an honorific form of *-te iru* is a hallmark of Kansai dialect, and is especially associated with Kyoto.

© Hirokane Kenshi / *Kachō Shima Kōsaku*, Kodansha

Has a gentle/innocent face

The playboy Kazamatsuri kindly offered to tutor Yawara at his apartment so she could do well on her college entrance exams, but of course he had ulterior motives. When his fiancée Sayaka came in unexpectedly and found them together, she accused Yawara of trying to steal Kazamatsuri. The soft-spoken heroine Yawara denied the allegation and then made a hasty exit. Here we see an example of ～ *kao (o) shite (-iru)* meaning "has a ～ face."

© Urusawa Naoki / *Yawara!*, Shogakukan

Sayaka: おとなしい顔して、とんでもないくわせもの
Otonashii kao shite, tondemonai kuwasemono
gentle/quiet face has astounding operator/troublemaker

です わ、あの コ。
desu wa, ano ko.
is (fem.) that girl

"She has a quiet face, (but) she's an utter trouble-maker, that girl."
"She looks innocent enough, but she's actually a real operator, that girl." (PL3)

ねっ、風祭さん。
Ne! Kazamatsuri-san
right (name-hon.)
"Right, Kazamatsuri-san?" (PL3)

- *tondemonai* can be used as a strong denial, "it's not like that at all," or as in this case, an adjective meaning "preposterous/outrageous/astounding."
- *kuwasemono* is apparently derived from *ippai kuwaseru* (一杯食わせる, lit. "make [someone] eat a helping" → "cheat/play a trick on").

Look on with indifference

Shima has just arrived in the Philippines on business. He and his contact are waiting for traffic to clear up when a small boy knocks on their window and tries to sell them a newspaper or cigarettes.

© Hirokane Kenshi / *Kachō Shima Kōsaku*, Kodansha

Kashimura: 知らん 顔 をしてろ。そんな の に
Shiran kao o shite-ro. Sonna no ni
don't know face (obj.) do that kind of (nom.) with/to

いちいち 取り合っている と キリがない ぞ。
ichi ichi toriatte-iru to kiri ga nai zo.
one by one are taking heed of if/when is no end (emph.)
"Don't pay any attention (to him). If you start responding to every one of his type, there'll never be an end to it." (PL2)

- *shite-ro* is a colloquial contraction of *shite-iro,* an abrupt command form of *shite-iru,* from *suru. Shiran kao o suru* literally means "do/make a don't-know face" → "pretend not to know/ignore/pay no attention."
- *shiran* is a contraction of *shiranai* ("don't know"), the plain/abrupt negative form of the verb *shiru* ("know").

99

A colloquial word for "face"

The word *tsura*, written with the kanji 面, is a slangy or colloquial word for "face." It's the word of choice when making disparaging remarks about someone's facial appearance. Here the oddball on the right was creeping around an old castle when he suddenly came face-to-face with the monstrosity on the left, giving them both a start.

© Toriyama Akira / *Dr. Slump,* Shueisha

Igor: きゅうにぶきみなツラを　だすな　よーっ!!
Kyū ni   bukimi na tsura o   dasu na   yo-!!
suddenly   weird   face (obj.) don't put forth   (emph.)
ビックリしたじゃないかーっ!!
Bikkuri shita   ja nai ka-!!
was startled   isn't it so
Don't suddenly stick your weird face out! I was startled, wasn't I!
"Don't go suddenly poking your weird face out like that! You scared me to death!" (PL2)

Frank: ヒトのこと　が　いえる　ツラ　かっ!!
Hito no koto   ga   ieru   tsura   ka!!
person's   thing (obj.) can say   face   is it
Is your face such that you can say things about other people?!
"You're a fine one to talk, with a face like that!" (PL2)

- a small *tsu* at the end of a sentence indicates that the sound is cut off sharply or emphatically.
- *bikkuri shita ja nai ka,* lit. "I was startled, wasn't I?" is a rhetorical question, and is actually a strong accusation: "I was really startled!!" → "you really startled me!!"
- *hito no koto ga ieru ka* is similar to the English "Who are you to talk?" Specific attributes, such as *tsura* in this case, can be added to indicate just what it is that gives the person no right to talk.

"Make a big face" = Act like a bigshot

Matsuda, who works for the sports paper *Nikkan Every,* is trying in vain to keep reporters from other papers from getting information that will hurt judo star Yawara's feelings.

© Urusawa Naoki / *Yawara!,* Shogakukan

Reporter 1: えっらそうに、日刊エヴリー!!　おまえんとこ　こそ　デッチあげの　記事　ばかりじゃねえか!!
Errasōni,   Nikkan Evurii!!   Omae n toko   koso   detchiage no   kiji   bakari   ja nē ka!!
looks/acts important   (paper name)   your place   (emph.)   made-up   (=) article(s) nothing but   is it not
"Like you're so important, *Nikkan Every*! You're the ones who run nothing but phony stories!" (PL2)

Reporter 2: 最初に　柔さん　のスクープした　からって、まだデカイ面　する　気　か!!
Saisho ni Yawara-san no   sukūpu shita   kara tte, mada dekai tsura suru   ki   ka!!
first   (name -hon.) 's   scoop   did because (quote)   still big/large face   do intention   (?)
"Just because you scooped the Yawara story first, you think you can keep on acting like some bigshot!?" (PL2)

Sound FX: ドドドッ
Do do do!
Thud thud thud
(sound of trampling feet)

- *omae n toko* is a contraction of *omae no tokoro,* "your place."
- *ja nē ka* is a corruption of *ja nai ka,* "is it not?" — a rhetorical question.
- *dekai tsura (o) suru* is the rough, slang version of *ōki-na kao o suru,* lit. "make a big face," which refers to someone who is acting superior/snobbish.

Show your face

Terada's boss is being transferred to Osaka, and has requested that the company not give him a going away party. But Terada has worked under him for eight years, and can't let him go without at least saying farewell.

© Furuya Mitsutoshi / *Bar Remon Hāto*, Futabasha

Terada: 部長、　おねがいします。
Buchō,　o-negai shimasu.
department chief　please
"Please, Chief." (PL4)

ちょっと だけ 顔 見せてください。
Chotto　dake kao misete kudasai
a little　only face　please show
"Just show your face for a minute."
"Just let me see you for a minute."
(PL3)

- *buchō* are the "department/division" chiefs of a company. Typical corporate structure has the *shachō* ("company president") at the top, followed by a number of *buchō*, under whom are *kachō* ("section chiefs").
- *o-negai shimasu* is a polite way of making a request or asking a favor.

Written all over your face

A few of the young boys have made a habit of frequenting a shop after school for a bite to eat. As it happens, the owner's daughter is cute and about their age. Today the boys run into a couple of their class rivals, who correctly deduce that the girl, rather than the food, is the real attraction.

Ryūnosuke: かくすな よ。
Kakusu na　yo.
don't hide　(emph.)
"Don't (try to) hide it." (PL2)

顔　に 書いてある よ。
Kao　ni　kaite-aru　yo.
face at/on　is written　(emph.)
"It's written all over your face."
(PL2)

- following the plain form of a verb with *na* makes a strong and rough command not to do the action, but since *yo* provides a friendly kind of emphasis, it softens the effect somewhat.

© Akiyama Jōji / *Haguregumo*, Shogakukan

BASIC JAPANESE through comics

Lesson 40 • The Many Faces of "Face" (2)

In Part 1 of our series on "face," we illustrated expressions that use the word *kao*, or its often derogatory cousin *tsura*. In most of those examples *kao* or *tsura* referred to the appearance of the physical face: handsome, smiling, troubled, innocent, an open book, and so forth. In this lesson, we will focus on expressions having to do with one's social face—which is to say, with appearances, honor, dignity, and reputation.

As with the English word "face," *kao* (and sometimes even *tsura*) can be used for the more figurative meaning of "social face." More common for this meaning, though, are the words *menboku* (面目) and *mentsu* (面子). You may sometimes hear these words in reference to physical face, but they are predominantly used when speaking of social face; they appear in expressions that essentially correspond to "lose face" and "save face" in English, as well as in other expressions of shame or embarrassment. The two words are pretty much interchangeable, but *kao* cannot always be substituted, nor can they always be substituted for *kao*.

Perhaps even more than in most of our lessons, the examples chosen here illustrate an important Japanese cultural trait along with language usage. We hope you'll note the degree to which each person's actions are perceived as affecting the reputation, or "face," of the people and organizations associated with him.

Awaseru kao ga nai—have no face to meet with

Hanazono has been spending all of his time at judo practice and neglecting his girlfriend Fujiko. Yawara, a mutual friend, meets him for coffee to urge him to see Fujiko and apologize, but Hanazono, ashamed that he has been doing poorly in judo while Fujiko is in top form, declares that he won't see her until he makes first string on the team.

Hanazono: 今 は 会わせる顔 が ない!
Ima wa awaseru kao ga nai!
now as for unite face (subj.) not exist/don't have
"As for now, I don't have a face to bring together with her."
"I simply can't face her right now!" (PL3)

- *awaseru* (more commonly written 合わせる in this expression) means "put together/unite," so *kao o awaseru* (顔を会わせる, literally, "put/bring faces together") is an expression for "meet." *Awaseru kao ga nai* (literally, "not have a face to bring together") is an expression used when you're too embarrassed or ashamed to meet/show your face to someone.

© Urusawa Naoki / *Yawara!* Shogakukan

Kao o tsubusu—crush a person's face

A blackmailer has approached Shima Kachō with compromising photographs of the wife of his colleague Hirai, as well as evidence that she was leaking company secrets. Shima advises Hirai to make a clean breast of the situation to the company and divorce his wife, but Hirai is concerned about the loss of face this would cause the man who served as go-between for his marriage.

Hirai: いや、離婚 は 出来ません!
Iya, rikon wa dekimasen!
no divorce as for can't do
"No, I can't get divorced." (PL3)

そんな こと を したら 仲人 を
Sonna koto o shitara nakōdo o
that kind of thing (obj.) if do/did go-between (obj.)

していただいた 井上 副社長 の
shite itadaita Inoue Fuku-shachō no
did-(for me) (name) co. VP 's

顔 を 潰す こと に なる。
kao o tsubusu koto ni naru.
face (obj.) crush thing will become
"If I did that, it would become a loss of face for Vice-President Inoue, who served as our go-between."
"If I do that, I'll bring shame upon our go-between, Vice-President Inoue." (PL2)

© Hirokane Kenshi / *Kachō Shima Kōsaku,* Kodansha

• *kao o tsubusu* (literally "crush [someone's] face"), or its passive counterpart, *kao ga tsubureru* (literally, "[someone's] face is crushed"), refers to situations where a person "loses face" or receives a blow to his or her dignity/reputation. Other synonymous expressions include *kao ni doro o nuru* ("spread mud on a person's face") and *kao o yogosu* ("soil/stain a person's face").

Kao o tateru—prop up a person's face

Several OLs from the Tōzai Newspaper decide to go out for *gyōza* ("potstickers"), and Yoshiko insists on choosing the place. When they get there, they see that it's a chain restaurant and are reluctant to enter—but they go in anyway, out of respect for Yoshiko.

OL: ま、 特別に よし子 の
Ma, tokubetsu ni Yoshiko no
(interj.) specially (name) 's

顔 を 立てる と するか?
kao o tateru to suru ka?
face (obj.) uphold/prop up (quote) do (?)
"Well, shall we specially uphold Yoshiko's face?"
"OK, let's do this as a special favor for Yoshiko, shall we?" (PL2)

• *tateru* basically means "make stand," and refers to putting something in an upright/vertical position, or propping it up so that it will not fall from such a position.

© Kariya & Hanasaki / *Oishinbo,* Shogakukan

• in many cases, *kao o tateru* would more literally mean "preserve/uphold (someone's) face/honor/reputation," but it can also be a simple matter of doing someone a favor.

Menboku ga tsubureru—face crumbles

The *o-chūgen* gift sent to the home of an important client at the request of Department Head Medaka has been returned: the General Affairs Section staff sent pet supplies for dogs instead of for cats. Medaka is furious because it represents a serious loss of face for him that the wrong gift was sent.

© Hayashi and Takai / *Yamaguchi Roppeita*, Shogakukan

Medaka: おかげで ぼく の 面目 は
Okage de boku no menboku wa
thanks to   I/me   's face/honor as for

まるつぶれ だ!
maru-tsubure da!
completely crushed is
"Thanks to your screw-up, I've lost face completely." (PL2)

Kachō: もうしわけありません。
Mōshiwake arimasen.
"I'm terribly sorry." (PL4)

- *okage de* means "owing to/thanks to/as a result of." It can be used either for giving credit or assigning blame.
- *maru-* is used as a prefix meaning "whole/complete"; when prefixed to the noun form of a verb, it means the action occurs/occurred "completely/fully." *Tsubure* is the noun form of *tsubureru* ("be crushed"), so *maru-tsubure da* = "is completely crushed." In an even more dire circumstance, *menboku maru-tsubure* can mean "(one's) reputation has been completely destroyed."
- *mōshiwake arimasen* is a very polite/formal apology. It literally means "I have no excuse" but is better thought of simply as "I'm terribly sorry" or "Please accept my deepest apologies."
- *o-chūgen* (the honorific *o-* is almost always included) refers to the custom of giving gifts at midsummer to one's boss, important business associates, and other social superiors, as a token of gratitude for favors received. The gifts themselves are also called *o-chūgen*.

Menboku ga tatanai—face will not stand

The magistrate is explaining why a samurai tried to hide the fact that his wife's death was a double suicide with her illicit lover.

Magistrate: かかあが 若い 男 と 姦通、
Kakā ga wakai otoko to kantsū,
wife (subj.) young man with adultery

挙句の果てに 心中 じゃあ よ、
ageku no hate ni shinjū jā yo,
ultimately   love suicide if it is (emph.)
"If your wife committed adultery with a young man, and ultimately killed herself in a lovers' suicide with him . . ."

Magistrate: 武士 の 面目 は 立たねえ よ な。
bushi no menboku wa tatanē yo na.
samurai 's face as for not stand (emph.) (colloq.)
"the honor/dignity of a samurai won't stand, will it?"
"it'd be pretty hard to uphold your honor as a samurai, wouldn't it?" (PL2)

© Akiyama Jōji / *Haguregumo*, Shogakukan

- *kakā* is an informal, old-fashioned word for "wife."
- *ageku no hate ni* means "ultimately" with a nuance of "on top of it all/to make things worse."
- *shinjū* refers to more than one person —usually lovers or family members— agreeing to kill themselves together.
- *tatanē* is a masculine/slang version of *tatanai*, negative of *tatsu* ("[something] stands"), the intransitive counterpart to *tateru* ("stand [something] up/uphold [something]") seen above.

Menboku o tamotsu—preserve face

The General Affairs staff of the example on the facing page arrange for a complete flea fumigation of the client's house to make amends for the mix-up with the pet supplies. A short while later, Medaka comes to thank the staff, saying the client was ecstatic over the improved conditions at home for his wife, who had been having an allergic reaction to her cats' fleas.

Medaka:

こっち も キミたち の おかげで
Kotchi mo kimi-tachi no okage de
this side also you-(plural) 's thanks to

面目 を 保つ ことができて 助かった。
menboku o tamotsu koto ga dekite tasukatta.
face/honor (obj.) preserve was able to-and was helped/saved
"Thanks to you, I've been able to preserve my honor. I'm very grateful." (PL2)

また 来年 の お中元 も あれで 頼む よ。
Mata rainen no o-chūgen mo are de tanomu yo.
again next year 's summer gift also that with request (emph.)
"Please go with that for next year's *o-chūgen*, too." (PL2)

• *menboku o tamotsu* is literally "preserve face/honor."
• *. . . koto ga dekiru* after the plain form of a verb essentially makes a potential form, "can/be able to (do the action.)"
• *tasukatta* is the plain/abrupt past form of *tasukaru* ("be helped/saved"). It's frequently used as an expression of gratitude.

© Hayashi and Takai / *Yamaguchi Roppeita*, Shogakukan

Menboku shidai mo arimasen—no face whatsoever

Long-time rivals Iwagawa from Nissei Television and Koizumi from the Tōzai Newspaper got into a public shouting match over the pedigrees of their cats, which culminated in the two challenging each other to a kendō duel. Their employers have arranged a dinner meeting to point out to them the damage their feud could bring to the companies, and they are persuaded to apologize.

© Kariya & Hanasaki / *Oishinbo*, Shogakukan

Iwagawa:

まことに どうも、 面目次第 も ありません。
Makoto ni dōmo, menboku shidai mo arimasen.
truly very much face/honor also/even have none
"I am truly very sorry." (PL3)

• *dōmo* is an intensifier, commonly used with expressions of apology/thanks/greetings/etc.
• *menboku shidai* is essentially a more formal and polite form of *menboku*. It almost always appears in the phrasing used here — though *arimasen* can become *nai* ("have none," PL2) or *gozaimasen* ("have none," PL4). Other possible translations are "I have no excuse/I can put no good face on it/I am truly ashamed."

Mentsu—honor

A banquet for 1,000 scheduled at the Hotel Platon has been canceled and moved to a rival hotel at the last minute, leaving the Platon with roomfuls of perishable food they can no longer use. Faced with the possibility of monumental losses, Manager Tōdō agrees to sell the food to the rival hotel, but this man from the sales department finds that hard to swallow.

© Ishinomori Shōtarō / *Hotel,* Shogakukan

Sales Manager:

それじゃ ウチの　面子　は
Sore ja uchi no mentsu wa
that if it is　our　face/honor as for

どう　　なる　んだ?!
dō　　naru　n da?!
what/how becomes (explan.)

"But in that case, what becomes of our honor?" (PL2)

- *uchi*, literally "inside," is often used to refer to one's own home/workplace.
- asking a question with *n da* is mostly masculine and usually sounds quite rough. In a case like this the question is essentially rhetorical.

Mentsu ni kakete—staking one's face

President Ōizumi Yūsuke of Hatsushiba Densen (a fictional company modeled on Matsushita) suddenly collapsed due to an apparent stroke while in a young woman's apartment. An ambulance is called, and after the doctor learns his patient is a VIP, he pledges to do his best with his hospital's reputation at stake.

© Hirokane Kenshi / *Kachō Shima Kōsaku,* Kōdansha

Doctor:

ハツシバ　　の　社長さん...?
Hatsushiba　no　shachō-san...?
(company name)　's　president-(hon)

わかりました。病院 の　メンツ　に　かけて
wakarimashita. Byōin no mentsu ni kakete
understood　　hospital 's face/reputation on staked-and

頑張って　　みます!
ganbatte　mimasu!
do our best-and　see

"The president of Hatsushiba . . . ? I see. Staking our hospital's name on it, we'll do everything we can!" (PL2)

- *ganbaru* means "exert efforts/work diligently/do one's best," and *mimasu* is from the verb *miru*, which, when added to the *-te* form of another verb, means "try and do one's best/do one's best and see."

Mentsu ni kodawaru—be particular about one's face

Section Chief Tomii of the Tōzai Newspaper publicly insulted some reporters from the Teito Newspaper in a fit of drunken excess after besting them in a golf match. He got carried away with his golf victory in part because Teito recently overtook Tōzai in circulation. Now Teito is threatening to have Tōzai's membership in the press club canceled and refuses to accept any apologies.

A: しかし、帝都さん も そこ まで 突っ張らなくたって ねぇ。
Shikashi Teito-san mo soko made tsupparanakutatte nē.
but (name-hon.) also there as far as even if don't push/insist (colloq.)
"But you'd think Teito wouldn't have to push things that far." (PL2)

B: 発行部数 日本一 の 新聞 と いう 面子 に
Hakkō busū Nihon-ichi no shinbun to iu mentsu ni
circulation best/most in Japan (=) newspaper (quote) say face/dignity on

こだわっている ん だろう。
kodawatte iru n darō.
are standing/sticking (explan.) probably/perhaps
"I suppose they're standing on their dignity as the paper with the highest circulation in Japan." (PL2)

• *tsupparanakutatte* is a colloquial conditional form of *tsupparu* ("push/thrust/insist"). The implied meaning is that "if they didn't push things that far, it would be OK."

• *kodawaru* means "to be very particular about/stuck on/hung up on" a certain point, so B is surmising that Teito is "hung up on" its face/honor/dignity as the leading newspaper.

© Kariya & Hanasaki / *Oishinbo,* Shogakukan

Mentsu o ushinau—lose face

In another contest between the rival newspapers Tōzai and Teito, the participants are food critics Yamaoka and Kaibara. Yamaoka has thrown the competition by first warning Ryōzō, who is in chef's training under Kaibara, to avoid the faux pas of serving horsemeat to a horse lover. Then Yamaoka deliberately commits the error himself. Ryōzō has come to thank Yamaoka.

© Kariya & Hanasaki /*Oishinbo,* Shogakukan

Ryōzō: 弟 から 全部 聞きました。
Otōto kara zenbu kikimashita.
younger brother from all/entirely heard
"I heard the whole story from my brother." (PL3)

山岡さん は、私たち 兄弟 のために
Yamaoka-san wa, watashi-tachi kyōdai no tame ni
(name-hon.) as for I/me-(plural) brothers/siblings for sake of

ご自分 の 面子 を 失う ような こと まで して...
go-jibun no mentsu o ushinau yō-na koto made shite...
(hon.)-self 's face (obj.) lose like thing as far as did-and
"In order to help my brother and me out, you went so far as to (deliberately) do something that (you knew) would make you lose face." (PL3-4)

• *ushinau* = "lose," so *mentsu/menboku o ushinau* is literally "lose face." *Kao* is not used with this verb.

BASIC JAPANESE through comics

Lesson 41 • *Kondo*—a word for all times

***Kondo* is written with the characters** 今 ("now," read *ima* when used by itself and *kon* in combinations) and 度 ("time/occasion," read *tabi* when used by itself and *do* in combinations), leading one to think that it may simply mean "this time" or "now." While this is indeed one of its most common usages, *kondo* proves to be much more versatile. It can refer to the past, present or future; it can be very specific, as in "the next (vacation, etc.)" or ambiguous, as in "some other time."

    The interpretation in each case depends almost entirely on the context. Here we illustrate some of the more common uses with examples from a selection of current manga.

This time

This man is extremely drunk and has come to the Hotel Platon late at night demanding a room. He is a ranking member of a corporation whose employees use the hotel frequently, and after being denied accommodations, he threatens to tell his company and other organizations of which he is a member to stop patronizing the hotel. One of the managers points out that the man did the same thing once before only to regret it the next day, after he had sobered up. The man, however, remains indignant and insists that he's really serious this time.

© Ishinomori Shōtarō / *Hotel,* Shogakukan

Man: 後悔 だ と!?
Kōkai da to!?
regret is (quote)

誰 が 後悔 など する もん か。
Dare ga kōkai nado suru mon ka!
who (subj.) regret something like do/have thing (?)

今度 は、 本気 だ!!
Kondo wa, honki da!!
this time as for true feeling/serious is/am

"Regret it!? Who's gonna regret it!? This time I mean it!!" (PL2)

• ~ *da to?* very roughly repeats something the other person has said, with the implication that the speaker is highly offended.

This time/now

The General Affairs Department of this company handles office supplies, maintenance and general support for the other departments. Here, the head of the General Affairs Department has just received a call that a door needs fixing.

© Hayashi & Takai / *Yamaguchi Roppeita*, Shogakukan

Dept. head: 今度　　　は　　会議室　　のドア　の
Kondo　wa　kaigi-shitsu　no doa　no
this time/now as for conference room 's door 's

具合　　が 悪い そうだ、有馬くん。
guai　ga warui sō da, Arima-kun.
condition (subj.) bad (hearsay) (name-fam.)
"Now they say the door to the conference room is messed up, Arima." (PL2)

- *guai ga warui* for people means "is sick"; for mechanical things it implies "is not working properly."
- *sō da* after an adjective or verb implies the speaker has heard about the action or condition from someone else.
- *-kun* is a more familiar equivalent of *-san*, typically used by superiors to address their subordinates in a company.

Next time

A Japanese salaryman stationed in Los Angeles and his girlfriend were confronted by this man a couple weeks earlier. At that time, he asked them for some money for food, promising to repay any amount he was given. The girlfriend decided to give him $100 instead of the $10 he asked for. In the scene below, he lives up to his promise, and it turns out that he is actually the president of a large company, posing as a homeless person.

© Hirokane Kenshi / *Kachō Shima Kōsaku*, Kodansha

"Homeless" Man:
ほら、借りてた 100ドル
Hora, karite-ta hyaku-doru
here had borrowed $100

返す　　　ぞ。　この間
kaesu　zo. Kono aida
am returning (emph.) not long ago

約束した　だろう?
yakusoku shita darō?
promised right?/didn't I?
"Here, I'm returning the $100 I borrowed. I promised you the last time, didn't I?" (PL2)

今度 出会った 時　に　返す　　って　な。
Kondo deatta toki ni kaesu tte na.
next time met time/when at will return (quote) (colloq.)
"That when I saw you the next time, I'd pay you back." (PL2)

- *kono aida* can variously mean "the other day/some time ago/not long ago/recently." In this case he's referring to the last time they met.
- the syntax is inverted; normal order would be *kondo deatta toki ni kaesu tte, kono aida yakusoku shita darō*. The quotative *tte* marks the content/specific nature of the *yakusoku* ("promise").
- horizontal writing in manga balloons indicates the character is using English or some other non-Japanese language.

Sometime (example 1)

This man has just stopped by to visit his daughter. As he makes his way out the door, he suggests that they go out at some unspecified time in the future for lunch or dinner.

Father: 今度　一緒に　メシ　でも
Kondo　issho ni　meshi　demo
sometime together　meal　or something

食おう　な、裕子。
kuō　na,　Yūko.
let's eat (colloq.) (name)
"Let's have dinner together sometime, Yūko." (PL2)

- *meshi* ("[cooked] rice") is also an informal word for "meal."
- *demo* literally means "or something/someone/someplace," but it's often used merely as a "softener" without carrying its literal meaning.
- *kuō* is the volitional ("let's/I shall") form of *kuu*, an informal word for "eat" used mostly by males.

© Yajima & Hirokane / *Ningen Kōsaten*, Shogakukan

Sometime (example 2)

Yawara and Fujiko are in Barcelona to compete in the judo event at the Olympics. It's the night before the competition begins and the two of them are strolling along the waterfront talking about the experience.

© Urusawa Naoki / *Yawara!*, Shogakukan

Yawara: バルセロナ、今度　は　ゆっくり
Baruserona, kondo　wa　yukkuri
Barcelona　sometime as for　slowly/leisurely

観光　で　来たい　ね。
kankō　de　kitai　ne.
sightseeing for want to come (colloq.)
"Sometime I'd like to come to Barcelona just to sightsee." (PL2)

Fujiko: ホント、なーんにも見てない　もん　ね。
Honto,　nānnimo　mite-nai　mon　ne.
truth/is true　nothing　have not seen (explan.) (colloq.)
"Really, we haven't seen a thing, have we." (PL2)

- *honto* is an informal *hontō* ("truth"); in colloquial speech it's often used to reply: "really/it's true/you're right."
- *nānnimo* is a colloquial *nanimo*, which is followed by a negative to mean "not anything/nothing." Lengthening the first vowel adds emphasis: "nothing at all."

Some other time (example 1)

The staff of the Tōzai newspaper company have just been invited by their boss to visit some people who raise pedigreed cats. The boss is an avid cat lover, but his enthusiasm for the adventure is not shared by Yamaoka, who suggests he might be able to go sometime in the future but not this time. It's clear in this case, however, that "maybe another time" really means "count me out!"

© Kariya & Hanasaki / *Oishinbo,* Shogakukan

Yamaoka: 俺、 また 今度 ね。
Ore, mata kondo ne.
I again another time (colloq.)
"Maybe some other time." (PL2)

Yamaoka: つき合ってらんねー。
(thinking) *Tsukiatte-rannē.*
can't be socializing/going along
"I can't be bothered going along (for such foolishness)."
"You gotta be kidding." (PL2)

- *tsukiatte-rannē* is a contraction of *tsukiatte-irarenai,* the "cannot be doing" form of *tsukiau* ("socialize/consort/go along with"). The expression is usually used with the feeling of "I can't be bothered going along/putting up with such foolishness." → "you've got to be kidding."

Some other time (example 2)

Judo superstar Yawara has just discovered that her application for taking a college entrance exam must be filed today, but just as she rushes out of the house to take care of it, her friend Matsuda (a sports reporter) appears. She gives a cursory "Hello" and dashes off, but he runs after her and tries to carry on a conversation.

Matsuda: 今日 は 取材 じゃないんだ けど!!
Kyō wa shuzai ja nai n da kedo!
today as for news gathering is not (explan.) but
"Today I'm not on assignment!" (PL2)

Yawara: それじゃ、 よけい 今度 に してください!!
Sore ja, yokei kondo ni shite kudasai!
in that case/then all the more another time to make it please
"All the more, then, please make it some other time." (PL3)

Sound FX: タッタッ
Ta! ta!
(sound of swift footsteps)

© Urusawa Naoki / *Yawara!,* Shogakukan

- *kedo* is literally "but," here implying something like "but doesn't that make a difference?/won't that persuade you to talk to me?"
- *shuzai* is a noun literally meaning "collection of data/materials," e.g. for news reporting purposes. When he says *shuzai ja nai* he essentially means he didn't come as a reporter — he's not after a news story.
- ～ *ni shite* is the *-te* form of ～ *ni suru* = "make it ～"; adding *kudasai* makes it a polite request, "please make it ～"

This one

As an employee of the prestigious Hotel Platon, Kinoshita is honor-bound not to divulge any private information he may learn about the guests. When he sees the fiancé of a friend come to the hotel with another woman, he must decide whether to honor the privacy of his hotel's guest or reveal the truth to his friend. He decides to tell her, and afterwards, his coworkers all agree he did the right thing, but one of them points out that he is responsible for creating a certain amount of unhappiness in her life. He acknowledges that it's true.

© Ishinomori Shōtarō / *Hotel*, Shogakukan

Kinoshita:

ええ、そう なんです。ホテルマン
Ee, sō na n desu. Hoteruman
yes that way (explan.-is) hotelman

として 鉄則 を 守れなかった
to shite tessoku o mamorenakkata
as rule/code (obj.) couldn't follow/honor

事 が、 今度の 件 を...
koto ga, kondo no ken o...
thing/fact (subj.) this matter (obj.)

"Yes, that's right. As a hotelman, the fact that I couldn't follow the (established) code (precipitated) this matter."
"Yeah, that's right! This whole thing happened because I failed to honor the hotelman's code." (PL3)

- ~ *to shite* is an expression meaning "as/in the capacity of ~ "
- *mamorenakatta* is the negative past form of *mamoreru*, the potential ("can/be able to") form of *mamoru* ("follow/obey/honor").
- *kondo no ken* could literally be rendered as "the matter of this occasion," but it essentially boils down to "this matter."

The next/upcoming

Totsuka, who works for a moving company, is speaking here to his young partner who grew up as an orphan in a rural area called Kusabara. Totsuka no longer has a family either, so he has no reason to go back and visit his hometown. He proposes that they make a trip to Kusabara together sometime, perhaps during their next summer vacation.

© Yajima & Hirokane / *Ningen Kōsaten*, Shogakukan

Totsuka:

隆ちゃん の 故郷 の 草原、 今度の
Takashi-chan no kokyō no Kusabara, kondo no
(name-dim.) 's hometown (=) (place name) next/upcoming

夏休み に でも 連れてって くんない かな?
natsuyasumi ni demo tsuretette kunnai ka na?
summer vacation during or sometime take [me] along won't you I wonder

"I wonder if you wouldn't take me with you to your hometown, Kusabara, next summer vacation?" (PL2)

- *-chan* is a diminutive most commonly used with children's names, but close friends use it among themselves at almost any age.
- *no* between two nouns can indicate that the two are the same thing: *kokyō no Kusabara* = "Kusabara that is (your) hometown" → "your hometown of Kusabara."
- *kondo no* often has the feeling of "the upcoming ," implying that "the next~" will come relatively soon/is not far off.
- *demo* (lit. "or something/someone/sometime/etc.") is again used as a "softener."
- *tsuretette kunnai* is a colloquial contraction of *tsurete itte kurenai* ("won't you take me along?")

Recently

Miyuki has just come across the picture of a man with whom the Tsurumoku Company recently established a contract. In this case, *kondo* is being used to refer to an event which took place in the relatively near past, or "just recently."

Miyuki: この 人 よ! 今度 ツルモク と
Kono hito yo! Kondo Tsurumoku to
this person (is-emph.) recently (name) with

専属契約 した 家具 デザイナー!!
senzoku keiyaku shita kagu dezainā!!
exclusive contract did/signed furniture designer
**"This is the man! He's the furniture designer
Tsurumoku Co. just signed an exclusive contract with!!"** (PL2)

Shōta: ボ... ボンジョルノ山本?
Bo- Bonjoruno Yamamoto?
(stutter) (name)
"B- Buongiorno Yamamoto?" (PL2)

- *keiyaku shita* is the past form of *keiyaku suru* = "to contract/sign (with)." Prefixing it with *senzoku* ("exclusive") makes it "sign an exclusive contract."
- the syntax is inverted; normal order would be *kondo Tsurumoku to senzoku keiyaku shita kagu dezainā (wa) kono hito yo. Yo* by itself at the end of a sentence can stand for *desu yo* ("is/are" + emph.).

From now on

The title of this manga is "Dr. Slump," a reference to the main character's constant blunders and mishaps. In this episode, the good doctor has decided to reduce the "ultrapowers" of his android creation, Arale, pictured here in the background, to those of a regular young girl. He hopes to avert the powerful collisions that result whenever she runs into him, and he boasts that now that he's made the adjustments, perfecting his creation, they'll have to call the manga "Dr. Perfect."

Dr. Slump: こんど から は この マンガ の タイトル が
Kondo kara wa kono manga no taitoru ga
next time from as for this manga 's title (subj.)

「ドクター・パーフェクト」になる ぞっ!!
"Dokutā Pāfekuto" ni naru zo!!
doctor perfect will become (emph.)

"From next time, the title of this manga will become 'Dr. Perfect'!"
"From now on, this manga will be called 'Dr. Perfect'!" (PL2)

- strictly speaking he's saying "from/beginning next time," since the name can't change until the next episode, but the situation is clearly one where we'd say "from now on" in English.
- *zo* is a rough, masculine particle for emphasis.
- although her name, アラレ, would normally be romanized as *Arare*, the author of this manga prefers the spelling "Arale."

BASIC JAPANESE through comics

Lesson 42 • *Wake—the reason why*

***Wake* is a handy noun** for a variety of uses, but unfortunately, the array of meanings and usages can make it difficult for beginners to grasp. *Kenkyūsha's New Japanese-English Dictionary* (known as the "Green Goddess" among translators) lists three basic meanings:

1) "Reason/grounds/logic" (e.g., *wake o kiku* = "ask the reason")
2) "Circumstances/situation/case" (e.g., *sō iū wake nara* = "if that is the case")
3) "Meaning/sense" (e.g., *wake no wakaranai* = "meaningless")

These three meanings occur in quite a number of idiomatic expressions, such as ～ *wake ga nai* ("would never [be/do]") and ～ *wake ni wa ikanai* ("can hardly/can't very well [do]"). The examples in this lesson demonstrate *wake*'s basic meanings, some of these idiomatic expressions, and two special cases any beginning student of Japanese should know: *iiwake* ("an excuse") and *moshiwake nai* ("I apologize").

Wake = reason

Shima is being chauffered to Bangkok. The driver of the car has proven to be integral to the success of Shima's business trip in Southeast Asia, and so Shima offers to help him get a job at his company's local factory. The driver declines, however, stating that he hates the Japanese.

© Hirokane Kenshi / *Kachō Shima Kōsaku*, Kodansha

Shima:
その　理由を
Sono　wake　o
for that　reason　(obj.)

きいても　いい　か?
kiite mo　ii　ka?
if ask　good/OK　(?)

"Is it OK if I ask the reason for that?"
"May I ask why?" (PL2)

- 理由 (normally read *riyū*) means "reason"; the use of these kanji help make it completely clear that *wake* here means "reason" rather than "situation/circumstance."
- *kiite* is the *-te* form of *kiku* ("ask").
- *–te mo ii* (or just *–te ii*) is the standard phrase for giving permission; adding *ka* makes it a request for permission: "is it okay if ～ / may I ～ ?"
- it turns out that the driver's father died at the hands of Japanese soldiers during World War II.

Wake = situation

Suzuki was planning on going fishing with Aya-chan, and was fantasizing about spending some romantic time alone with her. When Hamazaki appeared to say he was joining them, Suzuki couldn't conceal his disappointment. Now Hamazaki wants to know what's going on.

© Yamasaki & Kitami / *Tsuri-Baka Nisshi*, Shogakukan

Hamazaki: 俺 と行く のが そんなに 嫌な 訳? それとも
Ore to iku no ga sonna ni iya na wake? Sore tomo
I with go (nom.+subj.) that extent disagreeable situation or

彩ちゃん とふたりっきりで 行きたい 訳? どっち?
Aya-chan to futarikkiri de ikitai wake? Dotchi?
(name-fam.) with two-(alone) by/as want to go situation which
"Is it the situation that going with me is that disagreeable (to you)? Or is it the situation that you want to go with Aya-chan? Which is it?" (PL2)
"Is going with me that unpleasant? Or do you just want to go alone with Aya-chan? Which is it?" (PL2)

Suzuki: た、 他意 なんか あります か!!
Ta- tai nanka arimasu ka!!
(stutter) ulterior motive such a thing exist (?)
"D- does anything like an ulterior motive exist?"
"I have no ulterior motive at all!!" (PL3)

- *futarikkiri* comes from *futari* ("two people") + *kiri* ("just/alone") and is generally used to describe situations where two people are alone in a romantic sense.
- Suzuki's question is purely rhetorical; he is strongly denying that he has any kind of ulterior motive.

Wake = meaning

In the whimsical manga *Urusei Yatsura*, Ataru is wearing a boxing glove that moves on its own. The glove gets him into lots of trouble—for example, by making him place his arm around girls. Lum, his girlfriend, is not convinced that the glove is acting of its own accord.

© Takahashi Rumiko / *Urusei Yatsura*, Shogakukan

Ataru: おれ ではない、 この グローブ が 勝手に...
Ore de wa nai, kono gurōbu ga katte ni...
I/me is not this glove (subj.) on its own
"It's not me! This glove is (moving) on its own . . ." (PL2)

Lum: なに わけ の わからない こと いってるっちゃ!!
Nani wake no wakaranai koto itte-ru tcha!!
what situation of not understood things is/are saying (dial.)
"What incomprehensible things are you saying?"
"What are you talking about? That makes no sense!!" (PL2)

- some form of *ugoku* ("move") is implied at the end of Ataru's sentence.
- *wake no wakaranai koto* = "incomprehensible things/non-sense/gibberish."
- ending sentences with *tcha* is Lum's own personal "dialect" in *Urusei Yatsura*; here it's equivalent to the explanatory *no* used to ask a question.

> *Wake no wakaranai* as a modifying clause implies that the thing it modifies makes no sense, is incomprehensible, or is meaningless.

Verb + *wake da* = that means . . .

The man on the right, Fujita, is the former mail clerk at the Hotel Platon. He has just discovered that Inoue is the hotel's current mail clerk, which means that Inoue is his *kōhai* — i.e., his "junior/successor" in that position.

© Ishinomori Shōtarō / *Hotel,* Shogakukan

V + *wake da* literally means "the situation/case is that . . . ," but here it is more like "that means . . ." This expression is also frequently used to confirm what the other person has said or implied. Simply form a question by replacing *da* with *ka* or the more polite *desu ka.* For example, *iku wake desu ka?* ("does that mean you're going?").

Fujita:
すると 私 の
Suruto watashi no
then   I/me of
後輩 に なる 訳 だ!
kōhai ni naru wake da!
junior to become situation is
"Then the situation is that you are my *kōhai*."
"So that means you're my *kōhai*!" (PL2)

Inoue:
後輩!?
Kōhai!?
junior
"Your *kōhai*!?" (PL2)

- *suruto* is a conjunction, "in that case/then."
- *kōhai*, literally "comrade/colleague who goes after," is the counterpart to *senpai*, "the comrade/colleague who goes first." The terms apply to one's "junior/senior" status within a given group, such as at school, in one's company, in one's particular job within a company, or in various social organizations. Sometimes, though by no means always, the *senpai-kōhai* relationship is one of "predecessor" and "successor," as here. Always present is the implication that the *kōhai* must show respect to his *senpai* as a kind of "mentor," and the *senpai* should look out for his *kōhai* as a "protégé" of sorts — even if they've never met before.

. . . *to iu wake da* = that's the gist of it

Dr. Slump is talking with a video of his father, who is giving him a recipe for a love potion that will enable him to get a wife. His father finishes the explanation and asks if his son understands everything.

© Toriyama Akira / *Dr. Slump,* Shueisha

. . . *to iu wake* is a very useful expression for summing things up. The summary or explanation comes first, then *to iu wake* followed by *da/desu, datta/deshita* or *de* (the conjunctive form of *da/desu*).

Video/Father:
. . . という わけ だ。わかった か
. . . *to iu wake da. Wakatta ka?*
(quot.) situation/explanation is understood (?)
"That's the situation. Do you understand?"
"That's what you have to do. Do you understand?" (PL2)

Dr. Slump:
わかりました。
Wakarimashita.
(I) understand
"Yes." (PL3)

- *wakatta* is the plain/abrupt past form, and *wakarimashita* is the PL3 past form, of *wakaru* ("come to know/understand"). In an exchange like this, the answering *wakatta/wakarimashita* is essentially a "yes."

Verb + *wake (ga) nai* = There's no way!

This OL has the reputation of being a pushover. Her co-workers are constantly taking advantage of her inability to stand up for herself. Here one of them has given her a large task at 5:00 PM and insisted that she have it done by the next morning. She protests, but to no avail.

© Okazaki Jirō / *After Zero*, Shogakukan

OL: どーしていつも 前 の 日 に なって
Dōshite itsumo mae no hi ni natte
why always before of day at/to become

押しつける の よー!
oshitsukeru no yō!
push/force onto (explan.) (emph.)
"Why do you always wait until the day before to push work on me?" (PL2)

出来る 訳 ない じゃない!!
Dekiru wake nai ja nai!!
be able to do situation not exist does it?
"The situation of being able to do it doesn't exist, does it?"
"There's no way I can get it done!!" (PL2)

- *dōshite* is a colloquial *naze* ("why/how come").
- *natte* is the -*te* form of *naru* ("become"); here the -*te* form essentially makes *mae no hi ni natte* into an adverb for *oshitsukeru* ("push/force onto").
- *ja nai* is literally "is not" but here is being used as a rhetorical question, actually registering a strong complaint.

> ~ *wake (ga) nai* means "the situation of ~ does not/would not exist." It is often used in combination with potential ("can/be able to") forms, where it means "could never/can't possibly." Both with and without the potential it carries some of the feeling of the English "(there's) no way!"

Verb + *wake ja nai* = it's not that ~

Mr. Suzuki has just learned that his dinner partner was married once but soon divorced. He asks whether that means she has given up—implying that it's never too late to try again.

© Yamasaki & Kitami / *Tsuri-Baka Nisshi*, Shogakukan

Mr. Suzuki: もう 締めた 訳 じゃないん でしょう?
Mō akirameta wake ja nai n deshō?
already gave up situation/case is not (emph.) is it
"It's not the case that you've already given up, is it?"
"That doesn't mean you've completely given up, does it?" (PL2)

FX: ニコ
Niko (effect of cheerful smile)

- *akirameta* is the plain/abrupt past form of *akirameru* ("give up/resign oneself"). *Mō* is literally "already," but with *akirameru* it has more the feeling of "completely."

> Note the substantial difference in meaning between ~ *wake (ga) nai* ("the ~ situation doesn't/wouldn't exist" and ~ *wake ja nai* ("it's not the situation/case that ~").

Wake ga chigau = the situation is different

Kurata is a front desk clerk and Matsuda is her supervisor at the swank Hotel Platon. Matsuda is also the hotel's pool supervisor. When Kurata boasts about her friend the lifeguard, Matsuda jealously claims that lifeguarding isn't nearly as demanding as supervising the entire operations for the pool area. But when a visiting doctor explains how difficult it is to become a lifeguard and about the many responsibilities the job entails, Kurata gets to gloat.

© Ishinomori Shōtarō / *Hotel*, Shogakukan

Kurata: ネ ...ただの 責任者 と は、
Ne ... Tada no sekininsha to wa,
see? a mere person in charge from as for

ちょっと訳 が 違います!
chotto wake ga chigaimasu!
little situation (subj.) is different
"See? Compared to a mere supervisor, the situation is a bit different."
"See? It's a wee bit different from being a mere supervisor." (PL3)

Matsuda: な・る・ほ・ど・!!
Na ru ho do!!
I see
"I see." (PL2)

• using *chotto* ("a little") here is a case of deliberate understatement; she means "a lot."
• *chigaimasu* is the PL3 form of *chigau* ("is different"); ~ *to chigau* = "is different from ~."
• *naruhodo* expresses one's understanding of what has been said: "I see/indeed/really."

Verb + *wake ni wa ikanai* = I simply can't

Yawara is in a championship judo bout for the world title. Her opponent is determined not to lose and repeats over and over to herself that she must not allow that to happen.

Opponent: 負ける わけ に は いかない!!
Makeru wake ni wa ikanai!!
lose situation to as for not go
"I simply cannot lose!" (PL2)

Sound FX: ガ ガ ...
Ga Ga . . .
(effect of grappling)

> ~ *wake ni wa ikanai* makes a very emphatic statement that the action/event cannot be allowed to occur: "I simply can't/I can't very well/I can hardly/no way can I (allow) ~ "

© Urusawa Naoki / *Yawara!*, Shogakukan

Iiwake = (an) excuse

Katō is the lifeguard at the Hotel Platon mentioned on the previous page. Matsuda, the pool supervisor, is berating Katō for flirting with girls around the pool. In reality, the girls were simply flattering Katō because they were impressed with a dashing rescue he had just made.

Katō: あ、あれ。 あれ は あの 娘たち が...
A, are. Are wa ano ko-tachi ga...
oh that that as for those girls (subj.)
"Oh, that. Those girls were just . . ." (PL2)

Matsuda: 言い訳 など いりません!!
Iiwake nado irimasen!!
excuse such a thing don't need
"I don't need to hear any excuses!!" (PL3)

- *ano ko*, when written with the kanji 娘, means "that girl"; the suffix *-tachi* makes it plural: "those girls."
- *ii* is the stem form of *iu* ("say"), so *iiwake* is literally "stated reason" → "an excuse."
- *irimasen* is the PL3 negative form of *iru* ("need/require").

© Ishinomori Shōtarō / *Hotel*, Shogakukan

Mōshiwake nai = (I) apologize

Mōshiwake nai and its more polite form, *mōshiwake arimasen*, are standard phrases for apologizing. The polite form is the expression of choice when the occasion demands great gravity, as is the case here. Fujiko has discovered that she is pregnant and Hanazono, her boyfriend, is bowing low as they explain the situation to her parents.

© Urusawa Naoki / *Yawara!*, Shogakukan

Hanazono: 申し訳 ありません!!
Mōshiwake arimasen!!
excuse doesn't exist

すべて 自分の 責任 であります!!
Subete jibun no sekinin de arimasu!!
all/entirely my responsibility/fault is
"I have no exuse. Everything is my responsibility."
"I am deeply sorry. It is entirely my fault." (PL3)

- *mōshi* is the *-masu* stem of *mōsu*, the PL4-humble equivalent of *iu* ("say"), so *mōshiwake* is essentially a more polite form of *iiwake*, "excuse." Note, though, that the word *iiwake* cannot be substituted when making an apology.
- since *arimasen* is the PL3 form of *nai* ("not exist/not have"), *mōshiwake arimasen* is literally "(I) have no excuse." But usually it's better thought of as "I'm deeply/terribly sorry" or "Please accept my deepest apologies."
- *jibun* is used as a personal pronoun mostly by military personnel and male athletes.
- *de arimasu* is the PL3 form of *de aru*, a more formal equivalent of *da/desu* ("is/are").

BASIC JAPANESE through comics

Lesson 43 • *Tokoro*—knowing your place

In current usage, *tokoro* is generally written with kanji (所) when it means "place" in the physical sense; hiragana (ところ) is used for more abstract meanings, such as "point in time," "aspect," or "level."

The "point in time" sense is reflected in the most common grammatical patterns in which *tokoro* appears:
1) ～*suru tokoro da*   ("about to do ～")
2) ～*suru tokoro datta* ("was just about to do ～")
3) ～*shita tokoro da*   ("just did ～")
4) ～*shite iru tokoro da* ("currently doing ～")
5) ～*shite ita tokoro da* ("was just doing ～")

In this lesson, we illustrate examples of patterns 2 and 3 above, as well as an idiomatic use: ～*dokoro ja nai* ("simply not possible"). We also present a well-known conjunctive use, *tokoro-de* ("by the way").

First we begin with several examples that illustrate the various meanings of the word *tokoro* itself. (Note that *tokoro* is often contracted to *toko* in colloquial speech.)

Place

This is the most straightforward usage of *tokoro*: a physical location. These people are on their way to a cocktail bar located in a building that looks more like a run-down apartment complex than something open to the public.

© Kariya & Hanasaki / *Oishinbo*, Shogakukan

Man: こんな 所 に
Konna   tokoro ni
this kind of place in

いったい 何 が ある のか ね?
ittai   nani ga aru no ka ne?
(emph.)   what (subj.) exists (explan-?)(colloq.)
"What in the world are we going to find in a place like this?" (PL2)

• *ittai* is an emphasizer for question words: "(What) in the world?/(Where) the blazes?/ (How) on earth?," etc.
• asking a question with *(no) ka ne* is mostly reserved for males, and for superiors speaking to subordinates. When *no* is included, it shows the speaker is asking for an explanation of something.

A particular spot

In this example as well, *tokoro* means place, but in the sense of "part" or "spot" rather than geographical location. Mr. Nomura is explaining to his son, Tarō, how he hurt his head once as a child, and he points out the scar as proof.

© Saigan Ryōhei / *Yūyake no Uta,* Shogakukan

Nomura: ほれ、ここんとこ が ハゲてる だろ。
Hore, koko n toko ga hagete-ru daro.
look/see here of place (subj.) is bald isn't it?/right?
"See, this spot is bald, right?"
"See, I have a bald spot right here." (PL2)

Tarō: あっ、 ほんと だ。ケガしたところ だ。
A! Honto da, kega shita tokoro da.
(exclam.) true/real is got injured place/spot is
"Hey, you're right. (So) that's where you got hurt!" (PL2)

- *hore* (or *hora*) is used to focus the listener's attention on something, like "look/see/here."
- *koko n toko* is a contraction of *koko no tokoro,* an expression for "this spot here."
- *hagete-ru* is a contraction of *hagete-iru* ("is bald") from *hageru* ("become bare/bald").
- *kega* = "injury," and *kega shita* is the past form of the verb *kega suru,* "get hurt/injured."

> When *tokoro* is modified by a verb, adjective, or complete sentence, it's often best translated as "where."

Aspect

***Tokoro* can also mean** attribute or aspect. Here, Kume is talking to a friend who has just decided to quit his job as a salaryman and become a potter. The friend has worked as a salaryman for only one year, but he's afraid that the longer he works, the harder it will be to quit.

© Hayashi & Takai / *Yamaguchi Roppeita,* Shogakukan

Kume:
会社勤め なんての は、 半分、
Kaisha-zutome nante no wa, hanbun,
working at a company such a thing as-for half

惰性 みたいなところ が ある から なあ。
dasei mitai-na tokoro ga aru kara nā
inertia -like aspect (subj.) exists because (colloq.)
"(Because) working for a company has half/somewhat inertia-like aspects, doesn't it."

"Yeah, in some ways, when you work for a company, it's easy to get caught up in the flow." (PL2)

- *nante no wa* is a colloquial *nado to iu no wa,* which can be considered just a fancy *wa* ("as for").
- *hanbun* (lit., "half") means "somewhat/to a large extent" in this case.
- *dasei* = "inertia/force of habit/coasting/auto-pilot," and *mitai na* after a noun can be thought of as "~ -like," so *dasei mitai na tokoro* = "inertia-like aspects."
- *nā* or *nē* with a long vowel strongly expresses the speaker's concurrence/agreement/sympathy: "it really is so, isn't it?" → "I know what you mean."

> Depending on context, the more abstract uses of *tokoro* can mean variously aspect, character, manner, situation, circumstance, action, extent, etc.

A point in time

Hamasaki and Sasaki are trying to outdo each other by catching the largest fish. Sasaki has already caught a fish, albeit a small one, so he suggests they call it a day.

© Yamasaki & Kitami / *Tsuri-Baka Nisshi,* Shogakukan

In the examples on this page and the next, *tokoro* denotes a place/point in time or in some other linear progression.

Sasaki:
幸い 私 が 一匹 釣ったし、 適当な
Saiwai watashi ga ippiki tsutta shi, tekitō na
fortunately I (subj.) one-(count) caught (conj.) suitable
ところ で 切り上げます か、 浜崎ちゃん。
tokoro de kiriagemasu ka, Hama-chan.
point at quit/wind up (?) (name-fam.)
"Well, Hama, now that I've been fortunate enough to catch one, shall we find a good stopping point and head home?" (PL3)

Hamasaki:
エッ!?
E!?
huh?/what?
"What!?" (PL2)

- *tekitō na* = "appropriate/suitable/fitting."
- *kiriagemasu* is the PL3 form of *kiriageru,* which means to "stop/wind up/finish for the day," often with the added implication of "leaving/going home/going back to something else." *Tekitō-na tokoro de kiriageru* = "stop at a suitable point and go home" → "find a good stopping point and go home."
- the name 浜崎 is usually pronounced Hamazaki, but Hamasaki is from Kyūshū and insists on using the regional pronunciation.

A point in time/part

A group of people have gathered around the TV to watch a pro-wrestling match, but just as the good guy is about to get trounced, the TV station begins experiencing technical difficulties.

© Saigan Ryōhei / *Yūyake no Uta,* Shogakukan

TV: しばらく おまち 下さい。
Shibaraku o-machi kudasai
a while/moment (hon.)-wait please
"One moment please." (PL4)

Boy: なんだ, いい とこ なのに...
Nanda, Ii toko na no ni...
what good place/part even though it is
"Geez. Just when it's at a good part..." (PL2)

- *shibaraku* can refer to either a brief or an extended period of time, depending on the context. Here it is like "a moment."
- *o-machi kudasai* is a PL4 equivalent of *matte kudasai* ("please wait"), from *matsu* ("wait").
- *nanda* (literally, "what is this?") is often used as an expression of disappointment.
- ～ *na no ni* ("even though it is ～") often implies discontent or disappointment. The remainder of the sentence, specifically stating the cause of the disappointment, is often left out in colloquial speech because the situation makes it obvious.

Point in time/stage

The Hotel Platon has begun to receive one cancellation after another due to negative TV coverage. The employees don't know what to do and turn to Mr. Tōdō, the general manager. He remains calm, however, and insists that they shouldn't worry, at least not at this point.

© Ishinomori Shōtaro / *Hotel*, Shogakukan

Tōdō: 別に　　　　今　の　ところ　　は
Betsu ni　*ima no tokoro*　*wa*
[not] particularly now　= place/point as for

何も　　する　　気　　はありません。
nani mo suru　*ki*　*wa arimasen.*
nothing　do　desire/intention　as for　not have

"At this stage, I don't particularly intend to do anything." (PL3)

- *betsu ni* combines with a negative later in the sentence to mean "not particularly."
- *ima no tokoro* is literally "the place/point that is now" → "the present point/stage," or simply "this stage."
- ～ *ki wa arimasen* is the PL3 form of ～ *ki wa nai*, the negative form of the expression ～ *ki ga aru*, literally "have a desire/will/intent to ～"

Stage/level

In *Chinmoku no Kantai* (*The Silent Service*), a military thriller, the United States has already launched one attack on this Japanese commander's renegade submarine (the *Yamato*) and is making further threatening movements.

© Kawaguchi Kaiji / *Chinmoku no Kantai*, Kodansha

The expression *iku tokoro made iku* more commonly occurs in the potential form, *ikeru tokoro made iku* ("go as far as one can go"). It can refer either to physical/geographical movements or to movements through time/stages/levels, etc.

Kaieda:
ともかく　我々　は　日本　に　　戦後　　初めて
Tomokaku wareware wa Nihon ni sengo hajimete
at any rate we as for Japan at-(target) after war for first time

アメリカ という　敵　　に　　噛みつかせた んだ。
Amerika to iu teki ni kamitsukaseta n da.
America (quote) enemy to-(source) made bite/snap at (explan.)

"At any rate, for the first time since the war, we made our enemy the United States take a snap at Japan." (PL2)

行くところ　　まで　行ってもらう。
Iku tokoro made itte morau.
go place/point as far as will have them go
"We'll have them go as far as they will go."

"Let them escalate things to whatever level they will." (PL2)

- *Amerika to iu teki* = lit. "the enemy that is called America" → "the enemy that is America" → "our enemy the United States."
- *kamitsukaseta* is the past form of *kamitsuku* ("bite/snap at" or "fasten one's teeth into"). In cases like this where *ni* is used to indicate both the source of an action (the US) and its target (Japan), context must tell us which is which.
- *itte* is the *-te* form of *iku* ("go"); the *-te* form of a verb plus *morau* implies having someone else do the specified action — whether by asking them directly, or, as here, by simply allowing them to proceed with something they are already doing.

Just did/just occurred (~ *shita tokoro da*)

A past-tense verb plus *tokoro* can refer to the place where some action occurred in the past, as in the example at the top of page 121, but it also makes an expression for "(someone) just did the action/the action just occurred." In this scene, Roppeita and his section chief are taking a coffee break after checking in on the painting crew working at their office.

© Hayashi & Takai / *Yamaguchi Roppeita*, Shogakukan

Kurata: どう？ 進んでる か？
Dō? Susunde-ru ka?
how is/are progressing (?)
"How's it going? (Are they) making progress?" (PL2)

Matsuda: はい、今 経理 が 終わった とこ です。
Hai, ima keiri ga owatta toko desu.
yes now accounting (subj.) finished place/moment is
"Yes sir. They just finished (painting) the accounting (department)." (PL3)

- this *dō* would be spoken as a question, which makes it a colloquial "how is it?/how about it?/how goes it?"
- *susunde-ru* is a contraction of *susunde-iru* ("is/are progressing"), from *susumu* ("to advance/progress").
- *owatta* is the plain/abrupt past form of *owaru* ("finish"), so *owatta tokoro (da/desu)* means "just finished."
- *tokoro* is often contracted to *toko* in colloquial speech.

> Sentences like this often include verb modifiers like *ima* ("now"), *sakki* ("a while ago"), *saikin* ("recently"), *kyō* ("today"), *kotoshi* ("this year"), etc., but in some cases the "current/recent" nature of the action must be understood purely from context.

(Was) just now doing/just about to do (~ *suru tokoro da/datta*)

A non-past verb plus *tokoro* similarly can refer to the place where an action occurs or will occur, but it can also mean someone is "just about to do the action"—or with some verbs, "just now doing the action." Hagure, pictured here, is on his way to visit his son when he runs into him on the street.

© Akiyama Jōji / *Haguregumo*, Shogakukan

Hagure: 今 おまえの所 へ 行くところ だった のだ よ。
Ima omae no tokoro e iku tokoro datta no da yo.
now your place to go moment was (explan.) (emph.)
"I was just now going/about to go over to your place."
"I was just on my way over to your place." (PL2)

- *omae* is a relatively rough, familiar masculine word for "you," and *no* is possessive, so *omae no* = "your."
- *iku* ("go") is one of the verbs for which the non-past form + *tokoro* can mean either "just about to do" or "just now doing."

> *Datta* is the past form of *da* ("am/is/are"), but it is the tense of the verb <u>before</u> *tokoro* that makes the difference between the meanings "just did/just occurred" (past verb), "is just about to do" (non-past verb), and "is just now doing" (progressive verb, or in some cases non-past verb).

Simply not possible (~ *dokoro ja nai*)

Sasaki is talking to his mother on the phone. She called because he hasn't come to visit lately, but he explains that he just hasn't had the time.

© Yamasaki & Kitami / *Tsuri Baka Nisshi,* Shogakukan

Sasaki 忙しくて それ どころじゃなかったんだ。
Isogashikute sore dokoro ja nakatta n da.
busy-(cause) that place/position was not (explan.)
"I've been so busy, it simply wasn't possible."
(PL2)

- *isogashikute* is the -*te* form of *isogashii* ("be busy"); the -*te* form is here being used to state a cause/reason.
- *sore dokoro ja nakatta* is the past form of the expression *sore dokoro ja nai*, which emphatically states, "it is not a time/position/situation for that." The expression implies that the action referred to by *sore* ("that") might indeed be desirable, but, whether for lack of time or for some other reason, is out of the question/impossible/beyond one's capacity.

> *Dokoro ja nai* can also follow action nouns directly, as in *benkyō dokoro ja nai*, "I have no time (or energy/presence of mind, etc.) to be studying/I'm in no position to be studying."

By the way (*tokoro-de*)

At the very moment in *The Silent Service* that Kaieda is talking tough (the example at the bottom of page 123), US President Bennet is meeting with his top advisors to determine their next move. Partway through the discussion he realizes he needs some additional information about the situation.

© Kawaguchi Kaiji / *Chinmoku no Kantai,* Kodansha

Bennett:
ところで 「やまと」 が 核 を
Tokoro-de "Yamato" ga kaku o
by the way (submarine name)(subj.) nukes (obj.)
搭載した かどうか の CIA 報告 は?
tōsai shita ka dō ka no shii-ai-ē hōkoku wa?
loaded whether or not as-to CIA report as for
"By the way, as for the CIA report as to whether or not the Yamato took nuclear warheads on board (what did it say)?"
"Incidentally, what does the CIA tell us about whether or not the Yamato is armed with nuclear warheads?"
(PL3) ·

- *tōsai shita* is the past form of *tōsai suru* ("load/take aboard [a vehicle/ship/plane]," or when speaking of weapons, "arm").
- ~ *ka dō ka* after a verb makes an expression meaning "whether or not (the action has been/will be done)." *No* makes *Yamato ga kaku o tōsai shita ka dō ka* ("whether or not the Yamato loaded nukes") into a modifier for *CIA hōkoku* ("CIA report").
- the topic marker *wa* ("as for ~"), spoken with the intonation of a question, asks very generally about the status/condition/contents, etc., of what comes before it.

> *Tokoro-de* is a conjunction similar to "incidentally/by the way"; it can also be like "now" when that word is used to introduce a shift in topic or a new stage in the narrative.

BASIC JAPANESE through comics

Lesson 44 • *Shimau—ending it all*

On its own, the verb *shimau* ("finish/put an end to/put away/close") is fairly straightforward. When it follows the *-te* form of verbs, however, it brings to bear an array of nuances including completeness, regret, surprise, excitement, and impulsiveness. The abrupt past tense *shimatta* is often used alone as an exclamation, not to mean "I finished it!" but to express chagrin or dismay: "rats!/drat!/oops!/oh no!"

In colloquial speech, adding a form of *shimau* to the *-te* form of another verb usually results in a contraction, so it's a good idea to learn the pattern early on. For example, *tabete shimau* (食べてしまう, "eat completely") often becomes *tabechau* (食べちゃう); *katte shimatta* (買ってしまった, "bought impulsively") becomes *katchatta* (買っちゃった). If you remember that the *- te shima-* part contracts to *-cha-*, it should be easy to convert contractions back to their full forms.

Completeness

It is early summer, and Kōsuke has just finished jogging for the last time until the cooler weather of fall arrives. He is now on his way to a nearby temple, thinking it's also a good time to take care of some wood-chopping he'd promised to do.

© Maekawa Tsukasa / *Dai-Tōkyō Binbō Seikatsu Manyuaru*, Kodansha

Kōsuke:
和尚　　に　たのまれていた　肉体労働　　も
Oshō　　ni　tanomarete ita　nikutai rōdō　mo
chief priest by　had been asked　manual labor　also
今　の　うちに　　片づけてしまう。
ima no uchi ni　　katazukete shimau.
now of　within　take care of/finish-(completely)
"The physical labor I'd been asked to do by the priest, I would also take care of completely now."
I (decided) to also go ahead and finish off some physical labor the priest had asked me to do."
(PL2)

Sound FX:
カラン　カラン
Karan　karan
(sound of wooden *geta* on stone steps leading to temple)

- *tanomarete ita* is from *tanomareru* ("be asked a favor"), passive form of *tanomu* ("ask a favor").
- *ima no uchi ni* can mean either "now ahead of time" or "now before it's too late"—in this case meaning "before the weather gets really hot."
- *katazukete* is the *-te* form of *katazukeru* ("take care of/dispose of/finish"). You can think of the relationship between *katazukeru* and *katazukete shimau* as similar to that between "finish" and "finish up/finish off."

Regret

This man, a bank president, got into an argument with one of his clerks. They had been having an affair, and she was essentially blackmailing him. During the argument, he accidentally pushed her off the edge of a high building.

Man: 何て　　こと　を　してしまったんだ?
Nan te koto o shite shimatta n da?
what kind of thing (obj.) did-(regret) (explan.)
"What kind of thing have I done?"
"What have I done?" (PL2)

- *te* is a colloquial equivalent of the quotative *to iu*, so *nan te koto* literally means "a thing called/described/explained as what?" → "what kind of thing." *Nan te koto* often carries a feeling of shock or astonishment compared to the neutral *nani* ("what").
- *shite* is the *-te* form of *suru* ("do").
- the explanatory *n da* here is mainly for emphasis; asking a question with *n da* has a very rough or forceful feeling and is mostly reserved for male speakers.

-Te shimau/shimatta after a verb generally implies the action is/was regrettable, but it can also simultaneously convey any one of several related nuances: undesirable, unfortunate, irreversible, inappropriate, problematic, etc.

© Yajima & Hirokane / *Ningen Kōsaten,* Shogakukan

Surprise

Inokuma's French opponent in the Olympic judo finals was never expected to get this far, and came into the match shown here as a distinct underdog. When she wins a half-point and takes the lead, the crowd is stunned.

© Urusawa Naoki / *Yawara!,* Shogakukan

Referee:
はじめェ!!
Hajimē!
"Begin!" (PL2)

Sound FX:
ワーッ
Wā! (roar of crowd)

Commentator:
さ、　　さあ〜、　まったく　予期せぬ
Sa-　sā~,　mattaku　yoki senu
(stammer) (interj.) completely unexpected

試合　　　展開　　と　なってしまいました!!
shiai　tenkai　to　natte shimaimashita!
game/match development (quot.) became-(surprise)
"W- well, the match has taken a completely unexpected turn!" (PL3)

猪熊　が、なんと技あり　を　追う　　立場　　に!!
Inokuma ga, nanto waza-ari o ou tachiba ni!
(name) (subj.) (interj.) half-point (obj.) chase standpoint/position to
"Inokuma has most surprisingly been put in a position of chasing after a half-point."
"Who would have thought Inokuma would find herself a half-point down?!" (PL3-implied)

- *yoki senu* is a classical Japanese negative form of *yoki suru* ("expect/anticipate"); it is used in modern Japanese only when modifying another word.
- *natte* is the *-te* form of *naru* ("become"), and *shimaimashita* is the PL3 past form of *shimau*.
- *nanto* is an interjection that emphasizes surprise: "lo and behold/what a surprise!"
- *waza-ari* is a half-point awarded for a near but not quite complete execution of a throw in judo.

Completion + regret

Shirō's mom gave him ¥10 to buy a snack after school. He bought one of his favorite foods, a croquette, and quickly finished it off.

© Saigan Ryōhei / *Yūyake no Uta,* Shogakukan

Shirō:

チェッ、もう なくなっちゃった。
Che! Mō nakunatchatta.
(exclam.) already disappeared-(completely/regret)
"Shoot, it's all gone already." (PL2)

コロッケもっと いっぱい 食べたい なあ。
Korokke motto ippai tabetai nā.
croquettes more full amount want to eat (colloq. emph.)
"I really want to eat a large quantity of croquettes."
"I wish I could eat a bunch more croquettes." (PL3)

- *nakunatchatta* is a contraction of *nakunatte shimatta,* from *nakunaru* ("become lost/vanish/disappear").
- *korokke* is the katakana rendering of "croquette." When not otherwise specified, the typical Japanese *korokke* is a breaded, deep-fried potato patty, with a few bits of onion, vegetable, and ground meat mixed in.
- *tabetai* is the volitional form of *taberu* ("eat"). *Nā* emphasizes the desire.

> *-Te shimau/shimatta* often joins more than one nuance—most typically the feeling of "completeness" with either "regret" or "surprise/unexpectedness."

Completeness + surprise

Mamoru has fallen asleep on the shoulders of his older brother, Shōta, after a full day of going to the movies, eating ice cream, and walking around town. On the way home, Miyuki, Shōta's girlfriend, notices that all the excitement took its toll.

© Kubonouchi Eisaku / *Tsurumoku Dokushin Ryō,* Shogakukan

Miyuki: 寝ちゃってる...
Nechatteru.
is sleeping-(completely/surprise)
"He's gone to sleep."
"My, he's fallen fast asleep . . ." (PL2)

歩き疲れた の ね...
Aruki-tsukareta no ne.
got tired by walking (explan.) (colloq.)
"I guess he got tired from all the walking."
(PL2)

- *nechatteru* is a contraction of *nete shimatte iru,* from *neru* ("fall asleep"). *Shimatte iru* means "has done (completely/regrettably/surprisingly, etc.)."
- *aruki-* is the stem form of *aruku* ("walk"), and *tsukareta* is the past form of *tsukareru* ("grow tired"), so *aruki-tsukareta* is a compound verb meaning "grow tired from walking."

An unintended effect/result

Yawara was going to lose her judo match intentionally so she could bring an early end to the tournament. But when her male opponent came rushing at her (somewhat lecherously), her instincts took over. She flipped the man on his back for a win, much to her own surprise. Her teammate Hanazono (who wanted her to win) congratulates her.

© Urusawa Naoki / *Yawara!*, Shogakukan

Hanazono: まぐれ とは いえ、 よく やってくれたー!!
Magure to wa ie, yoku yatte kureta–!!
luck (quot.) say (emph.) well/effectively did-(for me/us)
"Though it was pure luck, you did well for us!"
"It may have been pure luck, but way to go!" (PL2)

Yawara: やっちゃったー!!
Yatchatta—!!
(I) did it-(unintended)
"I did (what I didn't intend to do)!"
"I beat him!" (PL2)

- ~ *to wa ie* is like "though it is/was/may be ~."
- *yatte* is the *-te* form of *yaru* (an informal word for "do"), and *kureta* implies the action benefited or fulfilled the desires of the speaker in some way.
- *yatchatta* is a contraction of *yatte shimatta* (from *yaru*).

> The two examples on this page are essentially variations of the "surprise" nuance. The feeling of surprise can come from something merely "unexpected," from something that goes directly counter to one's intentions, or even, as below, from something quite intentional, expected, and desirable but nevertheless surprising because of its boldness (or some other quality).

Excitement

It's Christmas Eve, and Nana can't believe Noriko had the guts to invite her handsome classmate to her family's holiday celebration.

© Tomisawa Chinatsu / *Katsushika Q*, Shogakukan

Noriko:
今年 は 同級生 の ケンタくん も ご招待しちゃった!
Kotoshi wa dōkyūsei no Kenta-kun mo go-shōtai shichatta!
this year as for same class student (=) (name-fam.) also (hon.)-invited-(surp.)
"This year I actually invited Kenta from my class to come, too!" (PL2)

Nana:
わあー、ごさかん!!
Wā–, go-sakan!!
(exclam.) (hon.)-lively
"Wow! Sounds serious!" (PL2)

- *shōtai shichatta* is a contraction of *shōtai shite shimatta*, from the verb *shōtai suru* ("invite"). The feeling of *shimatta* in this case is of surprise or excitement that she was bold enough to actually do it. The honorific prefix *go-* can be considered a feminine touch here.
- *sakan* ("lively/thriving") can refer to the liveliness of a person's work/trade or of a party, but a common idiomatic use refers to "lively/thriving" male-female relationships. The honorific *go-* is required for this idiomatic use.

An impulse: just do it!

The woman pictured on top has just convinced herself to buy an expensive blouse, even though she can't afford it. The salesclerk encourages her to go with her impulse.

<u>Customer:</u> 買っちゃう、 買っちゃう。
Katchau, katchau.
will buy-(impulse) will buy-(impulse)
"I'm gonna buy it! I'm gonna buy it!"
(PL2)

<u>Salesclerk:</u> 買っちゃえ、買っちゃえ。
Katchae, katchae.
buy it-(impulse) buy it-(impulse)
"Buy it! Buy it!" (PL2)

- *katchau* is a contraction of *katte shimau*, from *kau* ("buy").
- *katchae* is a contraction of *katte shimae*, using the abrupt command form of *shimau*.

Either the plain form or the abrupt command form of *shimau* can be used to express an impulsive desire or intent. It usually implies that the contemplated action is somehow unconventional, not what would be expected, or potentially problematic in some way, but you're not going to let that stop you—you're going to throw all caution to the wind.

Can't help oneself

Tabatake has a crush on Non-chan, but he recently discovered that she is dating another man. He is so depressed that he calls in sick and decides to visit her at the library where she works.

© Kubonouchi Eisaku / *Tsurumoku Dokushin Ryō*, Shogakukan

Tabatake: ボ…ボク 今日 仕事 休み で さ。来ちゃった。
Bo...Boku kyō shigoto yasumi de sa. Kichatta.
(stammer) I today work day off is (and) (colloq.) came-(no control)
"I...I have today off, you know, (so) I just came by..."
(PL2)

- *yasumi* is the noun form of *yasumu* ("rest") and in the context of work or school means "a day off/holiday."
- the particle *de* acts as a continuing form of the verb *desu*.
- *sa* is often used in colloquial speech to emphasize something the speaker thinks or knows is new to the the listener.
- *kichatta* is a contraction of *kite shimatta*, from *kuru* ("come"). The feeling *shimatta* gives here is that he knew maybe he shouldn't have come but somehow he couldn't help himself.

-Te shimau/shimatta often implies the situation was somehow beyond one's control: "(I did the action) in spite of myself/against my better judgment/even though I knew better," or "I just couldn't help but (do the action)."

Chagrin ("shoot!/drat!")

Shimatta, the plain/abrupt past form of *shimau*, is often used as an exclamation of regret, chagrin, or dismay, like a relatively mild expletive. The policeman in this scene was becoming high-strung and mean-spirited because of daily encounters with dangerous criminals. His commanding officer sent him to this small, quiet town in hopes that it would calm his nerves, but his menacing glances keep scaring passersby.

Policeman: しまった! また こわがらせちゃった。
Shimatta! Mata kowagarasechatta.
(exclam.) again made scared-(regret)
"Drat! I scared someone again." (PL2)

Sign: サクラヤ の パン
Sakuraya no pan
(shop name) of bread
Sakuraya Bakery

Sound FX: タタタッ
Ta ta ta!
(sound of fast-moving footsteps)

- *kowagarasechatta* is a contraction of *kowagarasete shimatta*, from *kowagaraseru* ("make [someone] be scared/show fear"), causative of *kowagaru* ("be afraid/show fear").

© Saigan Ryōhei / *Yūyake no Uta*, Shogakukan

Dismay ("oops!/oh no!")

Yōhei has just arrived at the monastery where he will spend a year training to become a Zen monk. When a senior monk catches him with a portable cassette player, he tries to explain, but the monk tells him not to talk back. Yōhei answers with an ill-timed "Yes, sir!" just as the monk adds an accusation: "Do you take your seniors for fools?"

© Okano Reiko / *Fancy Dance*, Shogakukan

Monk: こいつー!
Koitsū!
this guy/fellow
"You (twit)!" (PL2)

Yōhei: し、 しまったっ!
(thinking) *Shi- shimatta!*
(stammer) (exclam.)
"O- oops!" (PL2)

- *koitsu* is a contraction of *kono yatsu* ("this guy/fellow/thing"), a rough way of referring to another person. When directed straight at the person, it often feels like "you jerk/twit/idiot."

> English equivalents of *shimatta!* as an exclamation can range from "darn!/shoot!/rats!/oops!/oh no!" to stronger expletives that some people would find offensive; but in Japanese the word is not at all objectionable.

BASIC JAPANESE through comics

Lesson 45 • *Bakari*—more than nothing but

The easiest way to think of *bakari* in English is as "nothing but," but the word actually corresponds to a variety of English expressions, including "only," "all," and "a lot of." As usual, context is the key.

With verbs, *bakari* typically implies an exclusive or frequent action, but there is one prominent exception: when it follows a past-tense verb. Take the phrase *itta bakari* (行ったばかり), for example. *Itta* is the past tense of *iku* ("go"), so *itta bakari* looks like "went" + "only" → "only went." It actually means "just (at this moment) went."

The first three examples we present illustrate a sampling of *bakari* used with nouns. The next two pages show *bakari* in combination with verbs, and the last two pages give examples of more unusual grammar combinations as well as a handy expression of disbelief: *uso bakkari!*

Only/Nothing but

Tetsurō is wandering around a space colonization module looking for signs of human life. He has just entered what appears to be an engine room.

© Matsumoto Reiji / *Ginga Tetsudō 999*

Tetsurō: 機械　ばかり　か。
Kikai　bakari　ka.
machines　only　(?)
"So there's nothing but machines here, huh." (PL2)

• the question form is often used rhetorically when observing or confirming something for oneself, with the feeling of "So it's 〜, is it?"

All

This man has just met with the owner of a rival toy store and learned that the shop only sells toys of a peaceful nature.

© Saigan Ryōhei / *Yūyake no Uta*, Shogakukan

FX: ハッ
Ha!
(effect of sudden realization/comprehension)

Man: そう　か... なるほど。
Sō   ka ...   naruhodo.
that way (?)   I see/understand
"So that's it. I get it now."

そう　いえば、 土井玩具 の オモチャ は
Sō   ieba, Doi Gangu no omocha wa
that way if/when say (store name) of   toys   as for

そういうの ばかり だ　もん　な。
sō iu no   bakari da   mon   na.
that kind   only/all is thing/(explan.) (colloq.)
"Now that I think of it, the toys at Doi Toy Shop are all like that." (PL2)

- *ieba* is a conditional "if/when" form of *iu* ("say"), so *sō ieba* is literally "if/when you say that" → "now that you say that/mention it" or "that reminds me/now that I think of it."
- *sō iu* means "that kind of" and *no* is like "one" used as a pronoun, so *sō iu no* is literally "that kind of one" → "that kind."
- even without *sō iu no* to provide the meaning of "that kind," *bakari (da/desu)* after a modified noun can imply the objects in question are "all alike/of a kind."

A lot of

Sugita and Fuwa are interior designers currently working on a project for the father of Fuwa's high school friend. During the course of the project, the friend's younger sister ended up asking Fuwa to marry her. He turned her down, and now she seems to have disappeared. It's not the first time Fuwa's personal life has gotten mixed up with work.

© Hoshisato Mochiru / *Ribingu Gēmu*, Shogakukan

Sugita:
君 の まわり は その手の 話 ばかり だ な。
Kimi no mawari wa sono te no hanashi bakari da   na.
you   of surroundings as for that sort of   talk   only/a lot is (colloq.)
"As for around you, it's only that kind of talk, isn't it?"
"There seems to be a lot of that sort of thing going on with you." (PL2)

Fuwa:
すいません。
Suimasen.
(apology)
"Sorry." (PL3)

- *kimi* is an informal word for "you" generally used by males when addressing equals or subordinates.
- *te* is literally "hand/arm," but *sono te no* is an idiomatic expression meaning "of that kind/nature."
- in this case *bakari (da/desu)* implies that that kind of thing or talk "is abundant/frequent."
- *suimasen* is a colloquial *sumimasen*, which can mean either "sorry/excuse me" or "thank you," depending on the context.

Do only / Only ～

Yutaka is gazing at a picture of his late mother as a young girl. His mother was the founder of a new religion and had many followers. To Yutaka, however, she was simply loud and unattractive. He wonders why his father, himself quite handsome, ever married her.

© Yajima & Hirokane / *Ningen Kōsaten*, Shogakukan

Yutaka:
美しく　　も　　何と　　も　　なかった。
Utsukushiku mo nanto mo nakatta.
beautiful (emph.) [not] anything (emph.) was not
"She wasn't beautiful or anything." (PL2)

私の　　　疑惑　は　　深まる　ばかり　だった。
Watashi no giwaku wa fukamaru bakari datta.
my suspicion as for become deeper only was
"My misgivings only deepened." (PL2)

- *utsukushiku* is from the adjective *utsukushii* ("beautiful"), and *nakatta* is the plain/abrupt past form of *nai* ("is not"). *Utsukushikunai* = "not beautiful," and inserting *mo* essentially makes it emphatic: *utsukushiku mo nai* = "not even beautiful."
- *nanto mo* followed by a negative means "not anything"; ～*ku mo nanto mo nai* makes an expression for "not ～ or anything."
- *fukamaru* = "become deeper/deepen," and *bakari (da/datta)* after a verb means that is/was the sole action that occurs/occurred.

Do nothing but

While relaxing on one of the planets visited by the *Galaxy Express 999*, an interstellar train, Tetsurō was attacked by the son of the woman shown here. Her son wanted to steal his rail pass and travel to another planet with a big city, where he might have a chance to develop his musical talent into a career.

© Matsumoto Reiji / *Ginga Tetsudō 999*

Mother:　毎日　　紙　に　オタマジャクシの　行列　　を
Mainichi kami ni otamajakushi no gyōretsu o
everyday paper on musical note of parade/line (obj.)
かいて ピアノ ばかり ひいている 息子 だ　よ。
kaite piano bakari hiite iru musuko da yo.
write-and piano only is playing son is (emph.)
"(He) is a son who everyday writes parades of musical notes on paper and only plays the piano."
"Every day, my son does nothing but write music and play the piano all day long." (PL2)

- *otamajakushi* is literally "tadpole," but it's used as slang for musical note symbols, so a string of written notes can be called *otamajakushi no gyōretsu* ("parade of tadpoles").
- *kaite* is the *-te* form of *kaku* ("write").
- *hiite iru* is the progressive ("is/are ～ing") form of *hiku* ("play [a musical instrument]"). *Piano bakari hiku* means "play only/nothing but piano," but in this case the *bakari* also applies to the writing of scores, implying he devotes himself entirely to music and doesn't do other activities.
- the entire sentence up through *hiite iru* is a complete thought/sentence modifying *musuko* ("son"): "a son who ～"

Always (do)

Momo-chan's father owns a camera shop and recently hired one of her friends to work there. After a couple of drinks one evening, they get into an argument about artistic technique. Momo-chan tries to break it up.

© Saigan Ryōhei / *Yūyake no Uta,* Shogakukan

Momo-chan: もう いいかげんにしなさいよ、 二人 とも。
Mō ii kagen ni shinasai yo, futari -tomo.
already good degree to make it (emph.) 2 persons both
"Stop it! Both of you!" (PL2)

飲む と ケンカ ばかり して...
Nomu to kenka bakari shite...
drink if/when fight only/always do-(cause)
"You always fight when you drink." (PL2)

- *ii kagen ni shinasai* literally means "do/make (it) to a good/appropriate extent"—implying that a "good extent" has already been surpassed → "take it easy/that's enough/ stop it/cut it out."
- *to* after the plain non-past form of a verb can make a conditional "if/when" meaning.
- *kenka* is a noun for "fight/quarrel," and *kenka (o) suru* is its verb form (*shite* = -te form of *suru*, "do/make").

> With verbs in the -te iru form, *bakari* can come between -te and *iru*. For verbs without direct objects, it must come between: e.g., *naite bakari iru* = "is always crying/does nothing but cry." For verbs with direct objects, it can come either between the object and the verb or between -te and *iru*: *kenka bakari shite iru* or *kenka shite bakari iru*. Sometimes there's a subtle difference in meaning depending on whether the emphasis of *bakari* falls on the direct object or on the action of the verb; other times it makes no difference.

Just (did)

Sasayama has just finished berating Ama-chan (in the middle) for his philandering ways, including his liaisons with this bar hostess(Kazuho), to whom Sasayama has just been introduced.

© Yamasaki & Kitami / *Tsuri Baka Nisshi,* Shogakukan

Sasayama:
会った ばかり だが 気立て も いいし、
Atta bakari da ga kidate mo ii shi,
met just now is but disposition also is good-and

きちんとした 方 だ と お見受けした。
kichinto shita kata da to o-miuke shita.
proper person is (quote) (hon.)-judged
"I have only just met you, but you seem to be a very pleasant and respectable person."
(PL4-informal)

Kazuho:
あら、 嬉しい。
Ara, ureshii.
(interj.) happy/gratified
"Oh my! Thank you!" (PL2)

- *atta* is the plain/abrupt past form of *au* ("to meet"). *Bakari* after the past form of a verb implies "just now/ very recently (did the action)."
- *kichin-to shita kata* (*kata* is more polite than *hito* for referring generically to people) implies a person who is neat, proper, meticulous, or respectable in both appearance and manner.
- *o-miuke shita* is the plain/abrupt past form of *o-miuke suru*, a PL4 humble equivalent of *miukeru* ("take/judge [by appearances] to be").

For once

Ataru and his friends are at Ryūnosuke's house trying to coax Ryūnosuke's father out of his depression over losing his wife, Masako. The father is a notorious liar, and it is with some hesitation that they accept his story of how he and Masako met.

Ataru: さすがに 今度　ばかり　は　本気　らしい　な!
Sasuga ni kondo bakari wa honki rashii na!
even [he] this time only/for once as for serious apparently is (colloq.)
"This time, for once, he seems to be telling the truth!"
(PL2)

- *sasuga (ni)* is an emphatic expression that implies the action either fulfills or betrays one's expectation. Here, they would normally expect him to make up a story, but for once, "even he (with his reputation for lying)" seems to be telling the truth. See Basic Japanese No. 31 for more on *sasuga*.
- *honki* is strictly speaking a noun for "seriousness/sincerity," but often corresponds more closely to "serious/sincere."
- *rashii* shows that the speaker is making a judgment/conjecture based on something he has seen or heard: "apparently (is)/seems (to be)/(is) I guess": *honki rashii* = "seems to be sincere/truthful."

All/just because of

This man is mourning his lost wife, who passed away from an illness. He regrets that he couldn't afford what little medical help was available.

© Saigan Ryōhei / *Yūyake no Uta*, Shogakukan

Man: ゆるしてくれ... 志乃。
Yurushite kure . . . Shino.
forgive me (name)
金　が　ない　ばかりに
Kane ga nai bakari ni
money (subj.) not have only/just because
医者 に も 見せてやれず...
isha ni mo misete yarezu . . .
doctor to even couldn't show-(give)
"Forgive me, Shino. All because I didn't have the money, I couldn't even take you to the doctor, and so . . ."
(PL2)

- *yurushite* is the *-te* form of *yurusu* ("forgive"), and *kure* makes an informal/abrupt request or gentle command.
- *misete* is the *-te* form of *miseru* ("show"), and *yarezu* is a negative form of *yareru*, potential form of *yaru* ("give"), which after the *-te* form of a verb implies doing the action for someone else.

© Takahashi Rumiko / *Urusei Yatsura*, Shogakukan

Thought only/for sure

A serial murderer, pictured here with his first victim, is recounting to the authorities the chain of events leading up to his eventual capture. He was a frustrated insurance salesman, and when this woman, who had let him in only because it was pouring outside, laughed at the idea of buying insurance from him, he snapped.

Man: ボク は その 女子大生 が
(narrating) *Boku wa sono joshidaisei ga*
I as for that women's college student (subj.)

契約して くれる もの
keiyaku shite kureru mono
sign a contract -(for me) thing/case

と ばかり 思っていました。
to bakari omotte imashita.
(quote) only was thinking
"I thought for sure she would sign a contract."

Woman: アハハハハハハ
A ha ha ha ha ha
(laughing)

© Yajima & Hirokane / *Ningen Kōsaten,* Shogakukan

- *keiyaku* = "contract," and *keiyaku shite* is the -*te* form of *keiyaku suru* ("sign/ enter into a contract"). *Kureru* after the -*te* form of a verb means the action will benefit the speaker/subject.
- *joshidai = joshidaigaku,* "women's college"; *joshidaisei* = "student at a women's college."
- *sono joshidaisei ga keiyaku shite kureru* is a complete thought/sentence ("that student will sign a contract") modifying *mono* ("thing/case/situation"); the quotative *to* marks this as the content of *omotte imashita* ("was thinking," PL3 past form of *omotte iru,* from *omou,* "think").

Yeah, right/Gimme a break

Shōta went on a date with Mihoko, the sister of one of his roommates. After a number of drinks, they ended up in a "love hotel" (for couples, with hourly rates). It was Shōta's first time, and in his excitement, he bashed his head and passed out before anything could happen. Miyuki, another friend, has heard rumors about his escapades, and is not inclined to believe his account of things.

© Kubonouchi Eisaku / *Tsurumoku Dokushin Ryō,* Shogakukan

Shōta: だからぁ、確かに 女の人 と
Dakarā, tashika ni onna no hito to
therefore indeed woman with

ラブホテル で 一夜 を 明かした の は
rabu hoteru de ichiya o akashita no wa
love hotel at one night (obj.) spent (nom.) as for

事実 だ けど、やましい こと は 一切...
jijitsu da kedo, yamashii koto wa issai...
fact/truth is but shameful thing as for absolutely [not]
"What I'm saying is, although it's indeed true that I spent a night in a love hotel with a woman, absolutely nothing happened."

Miyuki: ウソ ばっかり!!
Uso bakkari!!
lies only
"Gimme a break!!" (PL2)

- *dakara* is literally "for that reason/therefore/that's why," often used idiomatically to mean "that's why I'm saying."
- *akashita* is the plain/abrupt past form of *akasu* ("pass/spend [a night]"). *No* turns the clause into a noun, and *wa* marks it as the topic: "as for spending a night in a love hotel with a woman."
- *yamashii* is an adjective but corresponds most closely to English "feel guilty about/be ashamed of."
- *issai* is used to strongly emphasize negatives: "absolutely (not/none)"; here the negative is left implicit: *yamashii koto wa issai* = "a thing to be ashamed of absolutely (did not happen)." In English we would simply say "absolutely nothing happened."

BASIC JAPANESE through comics

Lesson 46 • *Commands—part I*

Politeness can be a powerful tool. One of the most common ways to make a command in colloquial Japanese comes from the honorific verb *nasaru*, which is the PL4 equivalent of *suru* ("do/make"). When a command form of this verb, *nasai*, is added as a suffix to the *-masu* stem of verbs, the original polite verb takes on a whole new personality—expressing authority rather than deference.

When said in a sharp tone, *-nasai* can be quite forceful. Most of the time, however, it is used as a relatively gentle command, and sometimes it makes more of an invitation or suggestion than a command. There are also a number of everyday colloquialisms in which *-nasai* no longer carries any imperative meaning at all, such as *oyasumi nasai* ("good night") and *okaeri nasai* ("welcome home").

Even at its sharpest, *-nasai* has a more refined tone than the abrupt command forms which will be covered in the next chapter. We'd say it falls between PL2 and PL3 on the *Mangajin* scale of politeness levels. In other words, in spite of its origins, it's generally not appropriate in a situation where PL4 speech is required, because one does not normally go about issuing commands to one's social superiors.

Nasai (1)

The night before, Hamasaki had been looking forward to an intimate evening with his wife after putting their son to bed. The boy became sick, however, putting an abrupt end to Hamasaki's plans. Now, the next morning, Hamasaki is in a foul mood and scolds the boy when he tries to leave the table without finishing his breakfast.

© Yamasaki & Kitami / *Tsuri Baka Nisshi*, Shogakukan

Hamasaki: ちゃんと 食べなさい!!
Chanto   tabenasai!!
properly   eat-(command)
"Eat (your breakfast) like you're supposed to!"
"Finish your breakfast!" (PL2-3)

Sound FX: ガツ　ガツ　ガツ
Gatsu gatsu gatsu
(effect of eating quickly)

- *chanto* has a wide range of meanings ("duly/properly/perfectly/neatly/successfully/safely") but here essentially means "as you're supposed to."
- *tabenasai* is from *taberu* ("eat").

Nasai (2)

Takeda is normally a quiet, reserved man, but after a night of excessive drinking he loses his cool and gets into some trouble.

© Yamasaki & Kitami / *Tsuri Baka Nisshi,* Shogakukan

Policeman 1: 静かにしなさい。
Shizuka ni shinasai.
be quiet-(command)
"Settle down!" (PL2-3)

Takeda: ウルセーッ、バーロー、バーロー!
Urusē! Bārō, Bārō!!
noisy/shut up   fool   fool
"Aw, shut up, you jerk! You idiot!" (PL1)

Policeman 2: 連行   しよう!!
Renkō   shiyō!!
take to police station   let's do
"Let's haul him in!" (PL2)

- *shizuka* = "quiet," and *shizuka ni shinasai* is from *shizuka ni suru,* "be quiet."
- *urusē* is a rough, masculine corruption of *urusai,* which literally means "noisy/bothersome" but is used like the English expression "Shut up!"
- *bārō* is a slurred contraction of *baka yarō* (lit. "fool/idiot" + "guy/fellow"), which when directed at a person means "you idiot/S.O.B./jerk"—or worse.
- *renkō shiyō* is the volitional ("let's") form of *renkō suru,* which refers to taking a person somewhere forcibly. It's heard most often in connection with the police taking someone in to the station, but it doesn't imply formal "arrest" (the verb for which is *taiho suru,* 逮捕する).

Nasai (3)

Matsuda Kōsaku and Kaga Kuniko are reporters for a sports newspaper. Kaga usually takes the pictures, but Matsuda thought she wasn't going to show up today, the day of Yawara's championship judo match at Barcelona, because of a raging hangover from the night before.

Kaga:
カメラ を よこしなさい よ。
Kamera o   yokoshinasai   yo.
camera (obj.) hand over-(command) (emph.)
"Give me the camera." (PL3)

Matsuda:
加賀くん!!
Kaga-kun!!.
(name-fam.)
"Kaga!" (PL3)

© Urusawa Naoki / *Yawara!,* Shogakukan

- *yokoshinasai* is from *yokosu* ("hand over [to me]").
- *-kun* is a more familiar equivalent of *-san* ("Mr./Ms."). Among peers it's used mainly by males, but a superior may address or refer to either male or female subordinates with *-kun,* and more rarely a male will address or refer to a female peer using *-kun.*

A suggestion/invitation

***Nasai* can sometimes be** more of a suggestion or invitation than a command. The woman answering the door here recently discovered that her husband used her valuable NTT stocks to make an investment. Mr. Hame, the man at the door, is from the company that handled the transaction. He has come to explain the situation.

© Aoki Yūji/ *Naniwa Kin'yūdō,* Kodansha

Mr. Hame:
こんばんは。蟻地獄物産　の　破目　と　申します。
Konban wa. Arijigoku Bussan no Hame to mōshimasu.
good evening　(company name)　of　(name)　(quote)　say/be called
"Good evening. I'm Hame, from Arijigoku Products."
(PL4)

Woman.
ちょっと　入りなさい　　よ。
Chotto hairinasai yo.
a little　enter-(command)　(emph.)
"Why don't you come in a minute?" (PL3)

- *arijigoku* is literally "ant hell," the Japanese name for an "ant lion/doodlebug"—not a very likely name for a company in real life but obviously intended to tell us something about the way the company in this manga conducts business. *Bussan*, literally meaning "products/commodities," is used in the names of many Japanese companies, including those that deal mainly or exclusively in financial "products."
- *mōshimasu* is from *mōsu*, a PL4 humble word for *iu* ("say/be called").
- *hairinasai* is from *hairu* ("enter").

Offering advice: "You'd better . . ."

Nakamori is explaining to Sasaki that he is very lucky, for no matter who is named as the next president of the company, it seems that Sasaki will still be promoted to the position of *senmu*, "executive director." Nakamori warns him, however, to stay on the good side of both candidates.

© Yamasaki & Kitami / *Tsuri Baka Nisshi,* Shogakukan

Nakamori: だが、気を付けなさい　よ。
Daga, ki o tsukenasai yo.
but　be careful-(command)(emph.)
"But you'd really better be careful." (PL3)

Sasaki: ハイ...
Hai ...
yes
"Yes, sir." (PL3)

- *daga* is a conjunction like *dakedo* ("but"), only more formal.
- *ki o tsukenasai* is from *ki o tsukeru*, which means "take care/be careful."

Abbreviated to *na*

Takumi's younger brother is upset because the price of the notebooks he usually buys just went up, and he doesn't have enough money to buy one. Takumi urges him to ask their parents for a raise in his allowance to compensate for inflation.

© Kubo Kiriko / *Imadoki no Kodomo*, Shogakukan

Takumi:
じゃあ　　　さ、おこづかい
Jā　　　sa,　o-kozukai
in that case/then (colloq.) allowance

上げてもらいな　　　　よ。
agete moraina　　　　yo.
have [them] raise-(command) (emph.)

"Then you should get them to raise your allowance." (PL2)

- *jā* is a contraction of the conjunction *dewa*, "in that case/then/well."
- *agete* is the *-te* form of *ageru* ("raise"), and *moraina* is an abbreviated *morainasai*, from *morau* ("receive"); *-te morau* implies "have someone/get someone to (do the action)."

> The *masu* stem plus *na* is an abbreviation of the *nasai* command form (*agete moraina* = *agete morainasai* = "have them raise"). Note that this differs from the dictionary form plus *na*, which is a negative command (*agete morau na* = "don't have them raise").

In dialect

The Empire Finance Co., a shady loan company in Osaka, is about to finalize its loan to the failing Takahashi Construction Company. When Mr. Takahashi makes a mistake on the paperwork, Kuwata hands him a fresh form and tells him to take his time. Both men speak Kansai-*ben*, the dialect of the Osaka area.

© Aoki Yūji/ *Naniwa Kin'yūdō*, Kodansha

Kuwata:
社長、　　　おちついて、　ゆっくり
Shachō,　　ochitsuite,　　yukkuri
co. pres.　calm/composed-and slowly

書きなはれ　　や!
kakinahare　　ya!
write-(command) (colloq.)

"Mr. Takahashi, calm yourself and write slowly."
"Please relax, Mr. Takahashi, and take your time." (PL3-K)

Takahashi:
えらい　　　すんまへん。
Erai　　　sunmahen.
very much/terribly (apology)

"I'm terribly sorry." (PL3-K)

- *ochitsuite* is the *-te* form of *ochitsuku* ("settle/relax/become calm").
- *kaki-* is the stem form of *kaku* ("write"), and *-nahare* is the Kansai dialect equivalent of *-nasare*, which is the old form of *-nasai* (still occasionally heard in certain dialects).
- *ya* is used (typically in the Kansai dialect) at the end of commands, suggestions or requests to emphasize the speaker's desire that the action be done.
- *erai* basically means "admirable/worthy of praise and respect," but here the word is being used as an emphasizing adverb, to modify *sunmahen* (dialect for *sumimasen*, "I'm sorry") → "I'm terribly sorry."

Goran nasai

Nori-chan is explaining to her friend Kirita that her baby, who recently learned to crawl, always moves toward the camera when someone is about to take his picture.

© Kubo Kiriko / *Imadoki no Kodomo*, Shogakukan

<u>Nori-chan</u>: ほら、キリ太ちゃん、この カメラ
Hora, Kirita-chan, kono kamera
here (name-dim.) this camera

構えてごらんなさい　よ。
kamaete goran nasai yo.
hold/aim-and-see-(command) (emph.)

"Here, Kirita, try aiming this camera (at him)." (PL3)

カメラ に 突進してくる　わよ。
Kamera ni tosshin shite kuru wa yo.
camera to rush/move forward (fem. emph.)

"He'll come charging right at it." (PL2)

- *kamaete* is from *kamaeru*, which means "assume/ hold a position"; when the direct object is a tool, it implies "hold it at the ready," so with a camera it means "aim."
- *tosshin shite kuru* ("comes charging") is from *tosshin suru* ("rush/charge/dash forward").

> *Goran nasai* is from *goran ni naru*, a PL4 honorific equivalent of *miru* ("look at/ see"). *-Te goran nasai* urges the person to try the action and see what happens. In spite of its PL4 origins, because it's a command, *(-te) goran nasai* is appropriate only when speaking to persons of equal or lower status.

Gomen nasai

Saburō has just proposed to Sayuri. At first she is flattered, but then she realizes he's drunk and decides she can't trust his sincerity.

© Saigan Ryōhei / *Yūyake no Uta*, Shogakukan

<u>Sayuri</u>: こめんなさい。　私　帰ります。
Gomen nasai. Watashi kaerimasu.
(apology) I will go home

"I'm sorry, I have to go home." (PL3)

<u>Saburō</u>: 小百合ちゃん...
Sayuri-chan . . .
(name-dim.)

"Sayuri . . ." (PL3)

- *kaerimasu* is the PL3 form of *kaeru* ("return home"). *Wa*, to mark *watashi* as the topic of this sentence, has been omitted.
- *-chan* is a diminutive equivalent of *-san* ("Mr./ Ms."). It is most typically used with children's names, but close friends use it among themselves at almost any age.

> *Gomen nasai* is one of the most common ways to express an apology: "I'm sorry/excuse me/please forgive me."

Okaeri nasai

Yōhei has been living in Tokyo enjoying a carefree, fast-paced lifestyle as a college student and rock musician. His mother now welcomes him home to their small temple in the countryside.

Mother: お帰りなさい、俗物さん。
Okaeri nasai, zokubutsu-san
welcome home worldly person-(hon.)
"Welcome home, man of the world."

- *zokubutsu* refers to a "worldly/vulgar person" or a "philistine," so it's not a very nice name to call someone, but here it's a lighthearted reference to the fact that Yōhei has been pursuing worldly rather than religious pursuits.

> *Kaerinasai*, from *kaeru* ("return home"), would make a command, "Go home," but *okaeri nasai*, with the honorific prefix *o-*, is the standard greeting given when a person arrives home: "Welcome home/Welcome back."

© Okano Reiko / *Fancy Dance*, Shogakukan

Oyasumi nasai

Tokiko has had a fight with her husband and is spending the night at her former boyfriend Fuwa's place. The situation is a little awkward since Izumi is now living with Fuwa, and there is only one bed in the apartment.

© Hoshisato Mochiru / *Ribingu Gēmu*, Shogakukan

Tokiko: あたし　左っ側　じゃなきゃ
Atashi hidarikkawa ja nakya
I/me left side unless it is
眠れない から 先に 登る ねえ。
nemurenai kara saki ni noboru nē.
can't sleep so ahead climb up (colloq.)
"I can't fall asleep unless I'm on the left side, so I'll climb up first, OK?" (PL2)

Fuwa: じゃあ　ね、　おやすみ。
Jā   ne,   oyasumi.
well then (colloq.) good night
"Well, good night." (PL2)

Izumi: おやすみなさい。
Oyasumi nasai
good night
"Good night." (PL3)

> *Oyasumi nasai* (shortened to *oyasumi* in informal situations) is the standard "good night"; it can be used both for "good night" at bedtime and for "goodbye" when parting with friends late at night.

- *hidarikkawa* is a colloquial *hidarikawa* (or *hidarigawa*): "left side."
- *ja nakya* is a contraction of *de nakereba*: "if it is not" or "unless it is."
- *nemurenai* is the negative of *nemuru*: "sleep/fall asleep."
- *saki ni* implies doing the action "in advance/ahead of (something/someone) else" → "first."

BASIC JAPANESE through comics

Lesson 47 • *Commands—part 2*

There is nothing like an abrupt command for getting someone's attention. While a large part of the strength of any imperative is tone of voice, the abrupt forms generally carry more clout than the relatively polite *-nasai* forms introduced in the previous chapter.

In the examples below, we note how the abrupt command form is created for each of the basic verb types. We also show how *-te kure* and *-te kudasai* can be used as commands, and we introduce negative commands as well. Finally, we present two special cases: the *-tamae* ending, from the classical honorific verb *tamau* (給う, "grant/bestow" but not often used for these meanings in modern Japanese), and *irasshai*, from the honorific verb *irassharu* ("come/go/be in a place").

The abrupt command form (*ru* verb)

Shin-chan is not a morning person. He has a tendency to oversleep and habitually misses the morning bus. Today his mother has vowed to get him to the bus on time, but her first challenge is to get him out of bed.

Mother: さあ、 起きなさい、 しんのすけ!!
Sā, okinasai, Shinnosuke!!
all right/come on   get up/wake up-(command)   (name)
"Come on! Get up, Shinnosuke!"
"Come on! Time to get up, Shinnosuke!" (PL2-3)

Sound FX: ばっ
Ba!
(effect of sudden, vigorous action—here of pulling off cover)

Mother: 起きろ!! 起きろ!! 起きろ!!
Okiro!! Okiro!! Okiro!!
wake up   wake up   wake up
"Wake up! Wake up! Wake up!" (PL2)

Sound FX: がくん がくん がくん
Gakun Gakun Gakun
(effect of head limply bouncing back and forth)

- *okinasai* is a relatively gentle command form of *okiru*, "get up/wake up." We covered this kind of command form in Basic Japanese No. 46. It's made by adding *-nasai* to the *-masu* stem of the verb.
- *okiro* is the abrupt command form of the same verb.

How to make the abrupt command form depends on the type of verb. For *ru* verbs (most verbs ending in *-iru* or *-eru*), it's made by changing the final *ru* to *ro: okiru → okiro.*

The abrupt command form (*u* verb)

Sugimoto has been giving Shōta advice on writing a Quality Control Circle report. Now he leaves him to do it on his own.

<u>Sugimoto</u>: それじゃあ、オレ、用事　ある　から...
Sore jā,　ore,　yōji　aru　kara...
well then　I　business　exist/have　because/so
"Well, I've got some business to take care of, so . . ." (PL2)

正太、　頑張れ　よっ!!
Shōta,　ganbare　yo!
(name)　do your best　(emph.)
"Give it your best shot, Shōta!" (PL2)

<u>Sound FX</u>: がちゃ
Gacha
("rattle" of door latch)

- *sore jā* is a contraction of *sore de wa*, "in that case/then/well then."
- *ore* is a rough, masculine word for "I/me." *Wa*, to mark this as the topic, has been omitted.
- *yōji* = "business/an errand."
- *kara* ("because/so") here implies "so I have to go."
- *ganbare* is the abrupt command form of *ganbaru* ("try hard/do one's best"). *Ganbaru* ends in -*ru* but it's an *u* verb rather than a *ru* verb.

> For *u* verbs (all verbs not ending in -*iru* or -*eru*, and some with those endings as well) the abrupt command form is made by changing the final vowel *u* to *e: ganbaru* → *ganbare*.

Another *u* verb

The Sea Bat, Japan's first nuclear-powered sub, has just arrived at its underwater meeting place with US forces. The sub was built in cooperation with the United States, and this meeting was designed to test the new sub's performance in a mock battle, but Captain Kaieda has other plans. He begins by using his sonar to determine how many other subs are lying in wait for him.

<u>Kaieda</u>:
水測長、　　目標探信　ソナー　打て。
Suisokuchō,　akutibu　sonā　ute.
sonar chief　target exploring signal　sonar　transmit-(command)
"Sonar chief, transmit active sonar." (PL2)

- *akutibu* ("active") is given as the reading for the kanji *mokuhyō tanshin*. In this case, the kanji provide a definition for the foreign word written in katakana. We can assume that he actually said "*akutibu*."
- *ute* is the abrupt command form of the verb *utsu*, which can mean "hit/strike/shoot" or "transmit/send (a signal, telegram, etc.)."

> *Utsu* is an *u* verb, but note that -*tsu* changes to -*te* (not *tse*) because of the irregularity of the consonants for *t* row syllables: *ta-chi-tsu-te-to*. The *ts* sound occurs only with the vowel *u*.

An irregular command form

Sumitomo has just bought a boat. He is calling his younger brother, who no longer lives in their hometown, to invite him on a fishing trip.

© Yamasaki & Kitami / *Tsuri Baka Nisshi*, Shogakukan

Sumitomo: 帰ってきた とき は 乗せて やっかい
Kaette kita toki wa nosete yakkai
came home time/when as for will give ride because/so

早く 帰って来い!!
hayaku kaette koi!!
quickly come home

"Next time you're home I'll take you for a ride, so come home soon!" (PL2)

- *kaette* is the -*te* form of *kaeru* ("return home"), and *kita* is the plain/abrupt past form of *kuru* ("come"). *Kaette kita toki* can be "when you came home," but it's also used to speak of what will occur at some time in the future "when you have come home" → "when you come home."
- *nosete yakkai* is a dialect contraction of *nosete yaru kara*, "because I will give you a ride."
- *kaette koi* is the abrupt command form of *kaette kuru* ("come home"). *Kuru* is an irregular verb.

> *Kuru* ("come") and *suru* ("do") are the only two verbs formally classed as irregular in Japanese (though there are also a handful of special irregularities among otherwise regular verbs). The abrupt command forms of these verbs are *koi* and *shiro*, respectively.

-te kure command form

Tanaka-kun's boss is continually sending him on mindless errands. Here we have a good example of how the abrupt command form of the pattern *-te kureru* ("do for me") is used to give orders.

© Tanaka Hiroshi / *Tanaka-kun*, Take Shobo

Section Chief: 田中くん これ 郵便局 へ 出して きてくれ。
Tanaka-kun, kore yūbinkyoku e dashite kite kure.
(name-fam.) this post office to/at mail-and come back-(for me)

"Tanaka, take this to the post office for me." (PL2)

Sign: 課長
Kachō
Section Chief

Tanaka: ハイ!
Hai!
"Yes, sir!" (PL3)

- *dashite* is the -*te* form of *dasu*, which when speaking of mail means "post/send off."
- *kite* is the -*te* form of *kuru* ("come"), which after the -*te* form of a verb can imply "go do the action and come back." Adding *kure* after this makes a masculine command; a female speaker would say *o-kure* or use just the -*te* form, as in our next example.

> *Kure* is the abrupt command form of *kureru* ("give to me"), but when used with the -*te* form of another verb it sounds quite a bit softer than the abrupt command form of that verb. *Dashite koi* is a strong authoritarian command, while *dashite kite kure* can range from a gentle command to what we might call an abrupt request.

-te kudasai as a command

Judo star Yawara is being hounded by two reporters for a sports newspaper. Every time she turns around, they are hiding in the bushes somewhere snapping her picture, and she has finally had enough.

© Urusawa Naoki / *Yawara!*, Shogakukan

Yawara: いい　加減　に　して　下さい!!
Ii kagen ni shite kudasai!!
good degree/extent to make it please
"Enough already!!" (PL3)

Sound FX: パシャ
Pasha
(sound of camera shutter)

- *ii kagen ni shite* is the *-te* form of *ii kagen ni suru*, literally "make (it) to a good/appropriate extent"—implying that the "good extent" has already been surpassed. The various command forms of the expression are like "that's enough!/stop it!/cut it out!"

> *Kudasai* after a *-te* form usually makes a polite request, but it can be more of a command, depending on the tone of voice.

An abbreviated *-te kudasai*

Sasaki has to give a speech at a friend's wedding, but he is very nervous. His wife provides some words of encouragement as they prepare to leave for the banquet hall.

© Yamasaki & Kitami / *Tsuri Baka Nisshi*, Shogakukan

Wife: あなた、しっかりして!!
Anata, shikkari shite!!
you/dear be strong-(command)
"Get a hold of yourself, dear!" (PL2)

Sasaki: ああ、　大丈夫　です。
Ā, daijōbu desu.
(interj.) all right/no problem am/is/will be.
"Yeah, I'll be OK." (PL3)

- *anata* literally means "you," but Japanese women typically use it to address their husbands in the way English-speaking women use "dear/honey."
- *shikkari* is an adverb meaning "firmly/steadily/strongly," and *shikkari shite* is the *-te* form of the expression *shikkari suru*, meaning "be steady/strong" in the face of some challenge.

> The *-te* form of a verb by itself can be a short form of either *-te kure*, the relatively gentle command form, or, as here, *-te kudasai*, the polite request form. As in the above example, if it's said with enough emphasis, it becomes a command.

-naide: a negative command

Taeko is a computer genius. In high school, she and a number of other young students were hired to work for a large software company programming new computer games. Although the company made huge profits from their efforts, her peers were fired one after the other as they grew older and ran out of ideas, and now Taeko is the only one left. In her anger and frustration, she has climbed onto the roof of the corporate headquarters.

© Yajima & Hirokane / *Ningen Kōsaten*, Shogakukan

Man: 妙子!
Taeko!
(name)
"Taeko!" (PL2)

Taeko: 来ないで! それ 以上 近づくと
Konaide! Sore ijō chikazuku to
don't come that more than if approach

ここ から 飛び降りる わよ!!
koko kara tobi-oriru wa yo!!
here from jump down (fem. emph.)

"Don't come! If you approach any more than that, I'll jump!"
"Stop! If you come any closer, I'll jump!!" (PL2)

- *konaide* is a negative *-te* form of *kuru* ("come"), making a negative command or prohibition: "don't come."
- *chikazuku* = "approach/come near," and *to* makes it a conditional: "if you approach/come near."

> Verbs have two negative *-te* forms: *-nakute* and *-naide*. *-Naide* is used for negative commands.

A rougher negative command

Hiroko loves reptiles. She's a third grader and an *ijimerarekko* (いじめられっ子, "bullied child") because of her strange hobby. Nonetheless, she has decided to bring one of her many reptiles to school today.

© Okazaki Jirō / *After Zero*, Shogakukan

Hiroko: ほら、ロクベエ、こっちに 来て みい。
Hora, Rokubē, kotchi ni kite mii.
look (name) here to come-and see-(command)
"Look, Rokubē! Come see." (PL2)

Reptile: シャアア
Shaaa

Rokubē: ち... 近づくな!! バカ!!
Chi- chikazuku na!! Baka!!
(stammer) don't approach foolish/crazy
"D-don't come any closer! You're crazy!"
(PL2; PL1)

Other boy: ゲテモノ 趣味!!
Getemono shumi!!
bizarre thing taste
"You like weird stuff!!"
"Weirdo!!" (PL1-2)

- *kite mii* is a colloquial variation of *kite miro*, the abrupt command form of *kite miru*, "come and see" or "try and come" → "come over here."
- *chikazuku na* is the abrupt prohibition/negative command form of *chikazuku* ("approach/come close").

> Take note: The abrupt negative command form is made by placing *na* after the dictionary form of the verb: *chikazuku na* = "don't come near." When *na* is added to the *-masu* stem, it is short for *-nasai*: *chikazukina = chikazukinasai* = "come near."

Commanding with *-tamae*

Densuke and his wife Michiko are spending the day together shopping. They were about to buy some grilled snacks from a street vendor, but because it was the end of the day and the vendor only had two pieces left, Densuke suggested they wait to see if the price would drop. While they were waiting however, another person stepped up and bought them. Michiko jokingly scolds him, and he responds in kind.

Michiko: 責任　　　を　とり給え、キミッ!!
Sekinin　　o　toritamae,　kimi!!
responsibility (obj.) take-(command)　you
"You'd better take responsibility for this , young man!" (PL2)

Densuke: すいません、　課長!!
Suimasen,　　Kachō!!
I'm sorry　　section chief
"I'm sorry, boss." (PL3)

- *tori-* is the *-masu* stem of *toru* ("take").
- bosses often address their subordinates with a generic *kimi* ("you"), especially when they're angry.
- *suimasen* is a slightly less formal *sumimasen* ("I'm sorry").
- Densuke humorously calls his wife *kachō* ("section chief" → "boss") because her use of *-tamae* made her sound like his boss at work.

© Yamasaki & Kitami / *Tsuri Baka Nisshi*, Shogakukan

> The suffix *-tamae* attaches to the *-masu* stem of a verb to make a strong, authoritarian command.

A PL4 command

These two noodle shops were once a single establishment run by twin brothers, but the brothers had a fight and decided to each have their own shop. Unfortunately, they are across the street from each other, and the competition to attract customers is fierce.

© Kariya & Hanasaki / *Oishinbo*, Shogakukan

Brother 1:
さあ、どうぞ、　こっち　です　よ!
Sā,　dōzo,　kotchi　desu　yo!
OK　please this direction/side　is　(emph.)
"All right! Come on in! This is the place!" (PL3)

Brother 2:
こちら　が　本家　の　龍々軒。はい、いらっしゃい!
Kochira　ga　honke　no Ryūryū-ken. Hai,　irasshai!
this side (subj.) main house of　(name)　yes　come
"This is the original Ryūryū-ken Restaurant! Yes, come right in!" (PL2)

Banners:
元祖　　　手のべ麺
Ganso　　Tenobe-men
originator　hand-stretched noodles
"The Original Handmade Noodles"

- *dōzo* is used for "please" when urging the listener to do some action. In this case it implies "please come in."
- *kotchi* is a colloquial equivalent of *kochira* ("this direction/side"). *Kotchi desu yo*, literally "it's this side," implies "this is the place you're really looking for." Similarly, *kochira ga honke* emphasizes "this (side) is the original house."
- *honke* refers to the "main/head house" of an extended family or the "originator/original maker" of a product. *Ganso* is a synonym for the latter meaning.

> *Irasshai* is the abrupt command form of the PL4 verb *irassharu* ("come"); the verb is inherently polite, so even the abrupt form is polite. Shopkeepers shout *irasshai* both to welcome customers when they enter and, as here, to "command" pedestrians to stop by. In most respects, *irassharu* is a regular *u* verb, but this command form is irregular.

BASIC JAPANESE through comics

Lesson 48 • *Saying what you want*

In Japanese, how to express what you want depends on what exactly it is that you want. If you want to *do* something, you use the *-tai* form of the verb, which is created by adding *-tai* to the *-masu* stem (e.g., *taberu* ["eat"] → *tabemasu* → *tabetai*). If you want to obtain or possess something, you use *hoshii*. And if you want someone else to do something, you use *hoshii* with the *-te* form of the chosen verb (e.g., *tabete hoshii*).

These same forms are used when asking what your listener wants, but if you want to talk about a third person, there's a twist. Since you can't directly know that person's inner desires, talking about his or her wishes often requires the suffix *-garu*, which means "show signs of." *Tabetagaru* (from *tabetai*) literally means "he shows signs of wanting to eat," which for all intents and purposes boils down to "he wants to eat." By the same token, *hoshigaru* (from *hoshii*) literally means "she shows signs of wanting (the item in question)," which basically implies "she wants it." Even for the third person, though, you can get by without using *-garu* in certain situations, such as when you're quoting someone or making a guess about what he or she wants.

The examples we've gathered here also illustrate some of the other idiosyncrasies of these forms. We don't have room to cover all the permutations, but our selection should get you well on your way to expressing what you—and others—want.

Saying what you want to do: *-tai* form

Yukie is a *yuki-onna*, a supernatural creature in Japanese folklore. As in the folktale, Yukie has decided to marry a mortal man, which is unusual since *yuki-onna* are known for their propensity to kill men on sight. Yukie originally decided to become Tashiro's wife so she could have children and prevent her kind from becoming extinct. She now realizes that children are not what she cares most about after all.

© Okazaki Jirō / *After Zero*, Shogakukan

Tashiro: 雪江!!
Yukie!!
(name)
"Yukie!" (PL2)

Yukie: あんたと いっしょに いたい の よ!!
Anta to issho ni itai no yo!!
you with together want to be (explan.) (emph.)
"It's that I want to be with you."
"What I really want is to be with you!" (PL2)

- *anta* is a colloquial contraction of *anata* ("you").
- *itai* ("want to be [in a place]") is from *iru* ("be [in a place]")—the "place" in this case being "with you."
- ending a sentence with the explanatory *no* plus *yo* is mostly feminine; men would normally say *n(o) da yo*.

The *-tai* form of a verb is used to state what the speaker wants to do or to ask what the listener wants to do. It can also be used to speak of what a third person wants (or wanted) to do in indirect speech, explanatory and conjectural expressions, and in the past tense.

-tai form with a direct object

This boy has just been visiting a friend who has a pet rabbit. The rabbit recently gave birth to six adorable bunnies, and now the boy can't stop thinking about them.

Boy: 僕　も　ウサギ　を　　飼いたい　　なあ。
Boku mo usagi o kaitai nā.
I　also　rabbit (obj.)　want to keep/have as pet (emph.)
"I'd sure like a pet rabbit, too."
(PL2)

- *boku* is an informal "I/me" used by males.
- *o* marks *usagi* ("rabbit") as the direct object of *kaitai*.
- *kaitai* is from *kau*, which when written with this kanji means "have/keep/raise [animals]" (as pets or livestock).
- *nā* adds colloquial emphasis: "I sure wish ∼ ."

© Saigan Ryōhei / *Yūyake no Uta*, Shogakukan

> When a *-tai* form verb has a direct object, that object can be marked either with the standard object marker *o*, or with *ga*. In general, *ga* emphasizes the desire, while *o* throws the emphasis more onto the action involved. This means that in some cases only one or the other is appropriate.

Stronger desire: *-tai* form with *ga*

After the construction of a dam left her village buried under a reservoir, this old lady moved in with her daughter's family in the big city. The daughter is embarrassed by her mother's rustic ways and has asked her not to wear her usual shoddy clothes or work around the house. The mother soon longs for her old life in the country.

© Saigan Ryōhei / *Yūyake no Uta*, Shogakukan

Mother:
あーあ、また　　畑仕事　　が　やりたい ねえ...
Ā–a, mata hatake-shigoto ga yaritai nē...
(sigh)　again　field work　(obj.)　want to do　(emph.)
"Ahh, I sure want to do field work again."
"Ahh, I wish I could work in the fields again ..." (PL2)

- *ā-a* here is a sigh of woe; in other contexts it can be an interjection of disappointment or lament, like "Oh well/too bad/what a shame."
- *hatake* refers to "a cultivated field/farmland," so *hatake-shigoto* = "field work" of the agricultural type (not the academic type).
- in this case, *ga* is used instead of *o* to mark *hatake-shigoto* as the direct object, emphasizing the intensity of her desire. The desire is more intense because the situation is out of her control and she can't transform her desire into action.
- *yaritai* is from *yaru*, an informal word for "do."
- the elongated *nē* is like *nā* above: "I sure wish ∼ ."

-tai form with the particle dropped

Dr. Slump and his robot-creation Arale are visiting a coffee shop for the first time. The waitress thinks that Arale is Dr. Slump's baby sister.

© Toriyama Akira / *Dr. Slump,* Shueisha

Dr. Slump: ボクちゃん、　コーヒー。
Boku-chan,　kōhii.
I/me-(dim.)　coffee
"(As for) me, coffee."
"I'll have coffee."　(PL2)

Waitress: アラレちゃん　は　なに　のみたい?
Arare-chan　wa　nani　nomitai?
(name-dim.)　as for　what　want to drink
"Arale, what would you like to drink?"　(PL2)

- *-chan*, the diminutive equivalent of *-san* ("Mr./Ms."), can be used by adults among close friends, but its effect is humorous when used for oneself.
- *ga* or *o*, to mark *nani* ("what") as the direct object of *nomitai* ("want to drink," from *nomu*, "drink"), has been omitted, as is often done in colloquial speech.
- although her name, アラレ, would normally be romanized as *Arare*, the author of this manga prefers the spelling "Arale."

When you *don't* want to do it

Michiko is cleaning Densuke's ears, a common, and somewhat intimate, practice between husband and wife. Densuke is enjoying it so much, he doesn't feel like doing anything else.

© Yamasaki & Kitami / *Tsuri Baka Nisshi,* Shogakukan

Michiko: ここ　ね、コチョコチョコチョ。
Koko　ne,　kocho kocho kocho.
this place/here　(colloq.)　tickle　tickle　tickle
"This spot here, right? Koochie, koochie."　(PL2)

Densuke: いい!! もう　会社　なんか 行きたくない!!
Ii!!　Mō　kaisha　nanka　ikitakunai!!
good　(emph.)　company/work　a thing like　don't want to go
"That feels great! I don't want to go to work anymore!"
"Ahh, this is heaven! Forget work!"　(PL2)

- *kocho-kocho* is not just a manga FX word for "tickling"; as in this example, it's usually actually spoken when tickling someone, and *kocho-kocho to* is regularly used as an adverb when describing a tickling action.
- *mō* is literally "now/already," but when followed by a negative it implies "no longer ~ /not ~ anymore."
- *nanka* belittles what comes before it, creating a nuance of "as for the likes of work, ~" or "as for something so trifling as work, ~ ."
- *ikitakunai* is the negative of *ikitai*, from *iku* ("go").

> *-Tai* essentially conjugates like an adjective, so its negative form is *-takunai*, its past form is *-takatta*, and its past negative form is *-takunakatta.*

Saying what you want to have: *hoshii*

When you want to *obtain* or *possess* something instead of *do* something, the word to use is *hoshii*. Here, immigrant laborer Garcia meets an unusual salesman on the street and is drawn into a conversation with him.

© Takeuchi Akira / *Garcia-kun*, Futabasha

Man: 願い を ひとつ だけ　かなえてやろう。
Negai o hitotsu dake　kanaete yarō.
wish (obj.) one only/just shall grant-(for you)
"I'll grant you just one wish." (PL2)

Garcia: 日本人　　　の　友達　が 欲しい。
Nihonjin　　no tomodachi ga　hoshii.
Japanese person who is friend (subj.) want
"I want a Japanese friend." (PL2)

- *negai* is a noun form of *negau* ("make a request/ask a favor") → "a request/wish."
- *kanaete* is the *-te* form of *kanaeru* ("grant [a request/ wish]"), and *yarō* is the volitional ("I shall") form of *yaru*, which after the *-te* form of a verb implies doing that action for someone else.
- *no* here implies that *Nihonjin* ("Japanese person") and *tomodachi* ("friend") are the same thing: "friend who is a Japanese person" → "Japanese friend."

> *Hoshii* is used to state what the speaker wants or ask what the listener wants. It can also be used to speak of what a third person wants in indirect speech, explanatory and conjectural expressions, and in the past tense. The word takes what's known as "the *wa-ga* construction": the person who wants is marked with *wa* (though this part is often implicit and doesn't need to be stated), and the thing wanted (i.e., the direct object) is marked with *ga*. Unlike with *-tai*, you cannot use *o*.

Hoshii with particle dropped

Haibara has been living alone for a long time. A woman he met recently has set him to thinking.

© Aoki Yūji / *Naniwa Kin'yūdō*, Kodansha

Haibara: 嫁さん　　　欲しい なー。
Yome-san　　hoshii　nā.
bride/wife-(hon.) want (colloq.)
"I sure wish I had a wife." (PL2)

- *ga*, to mark *yome-san* as the object desired, has been omitted. This often occurs in colloquial speech.
- as one of several words for "wife," each of which has its own special use, *yome* (or *yome-san*) tends to be used when speaking of brides or recently married wives. *Yome* can also mean "daughter-in-law"; with this usage, a middle-aged woman married for ten years or more may still be referred to as so-and-so's *o-yome-san* in a multi-generation household, as long as the mother-in-law is alive. Finally, *yome* can mean simply "wife," a usage especially common in the Kansai area.

When you want someone else to do something: *-te hoshii*

Hirai is being blackmailed by someone who has photos of his wife having sex with another man. The blackmailer is threatening to make the pictures public and ruin his reputation at his company. Hirai is now confronting his wife with the evidence.

© Hirokane Kenshi / *Kachō Shima Kōsaku*, Kodansha

Hirai: おまえ に、まず、この 写真 を 見て 欲しい。
Omae ni, mazu, kono shashin o mite hoshii.
you (i.o.) first these photos (obj.) want [you] to look at
"First, I'd like you to take a look at these pictures."
(PL2)

- *omae* is an informal, mostly masculine word for "you."
- *ni* marks the person whom the speaker would like to have perform the desired action.
- *o* marks *shashin* ("photograph") as the direct object of *mite hoshii* (from *miru*, "look at").

> The *-te* form of a verb plus *hoshii* is for stating what you want someone else to do or asking what your listener wants someone else to do. The direct object is marked with *o*. This pattern cannot be used to state what you yourself want to do. Also, you should avoid using this form with your superiors. For them you need to say *-te itadakitai*—i.e., use the *-tai* form of *itadaku*, the word for "receive (from a social superior)."

The negative form of *hoshii*

A rumor is circulating among the staff at the Hotel Platon that their beloved hotel manager, Mr. Tōdō, may have to quit due to complaints from an important patron.

© Ishinomori Shōtaro / *Hotel*, Shogakukan

Housekeeper: あたし だって、
Atashi datte,
I/me too/either

辞めて ほしくない けど さァ...
yamete hoshikunai kedo sā, ...
don't want [him] to quit but (colloq.)
"I, too, don't want him to quit, but, you know . . ."
"I don't want him to quit either . . ."
(PL2)

- *atashi* is a variation of *watashi* ("I/me"), used mostly by female speakers.
- *datte* is a colloquial *mo*, meaning "too/also," or in combination with a negative, "(not) either."
- *yamete* is the *-te* form of *yameru* ("quit work/ resign," when written with this kanji), and *hoshikunai* is the negative form of *hoshii*. *Yamete hoshikunai* = "don't want (someone) to quit"—the someone in this case being Tōdō.
- the particle *sa* or *sā* in the middle of a sentence is often like the colloquial English pause words "like/you know."

> *Hoshii*, like *-tai*, conjugates as an adjective, so its negative form is *hoshikunai*, its past form is *hoshikatta*, and its past negative form is *hoshikunakatta*. These forms are the same whether *hoshii* stands alone or comes after the *-te* form of a verb.

When a third person wants to do something: *-tagaru*

Kat-chan's friends were playing an exciting game when he walked by. They asked him to join in, but, much to their surprise, he glumly said he didn't feel like it. They use a *-tagaru* form to comment on his unusual behavior of late.

© Saigan Ryōhei / *Yūyake no Uta,* Shogakukan

Boy 1:
勝ちゃん、この頃　元気　ない　なあ。
Kat-chan, kono goro genki nai nā.
(name-dim.) these days energy/vitality not have (emph.)
"Kat-chan is gloomy these days, isn't he."
"Kat-chan just isn't himself these days." (PL2)

Boy 2:
いつも　なら　まっ先に　やりたがる　のに。
Itsumo nara, massaki ni yaritagaru noni.
always/usual if it is very first [he] wants to do even though
"Even though he's usually the first one to want to play."
"Normally he's the first one to want to play." (PL2)

- *genki* is a noun referring to both good spirits and good health; *genki (ga) nai* means a person lacks vitality, or looks or acts depressed.
- *itsumo* = "always," and *nara* = "if it is," so *itsumo nara* is literally, "if it is always" → "normally/usually."
- *massaki ni* is an emphatic form of *saki ni* ("first/before") → "the very first/before anyone else."
- *yari-* is the stem form of *yaru* ("do," or when speaking of a game, "play").

> The suffix *-garu* attaches to *-tai* and *hoshii* and certain other adjectives of feeling to create verbs that mean "show signs of (being) ∼." These are used to speak of how a third person is feeling. Direct objects are marked with *o* for both *-tagaru* and *hoshigaru*. Since these forms describe what the person feels based on some surface manifestation of that feeling, they can also be used in the second person; but they cannot be used in the first person except to say that someone else observed a certain show of feeling on the speaker's part.

When a third person wants to have something: *hoshigaru*

Ippei (off panel) is staying at his mother's house in the countryside to recuperate from an ongoing illness. A shrine outside the room where he lies bedridden is dedicated to the spirit of a fox, an animal he had never seen before tonight.

© Saigan Ryōhei / *Yūyake no Uta,* Shogakukan

Ippei: そう　か、あれ　が　きつね　だ　な。
Sō ka, are ga kitsune da na.
that way (?) that (subj.) fox is (colloq.)
"Ahaa, so that's a fox." (PL2)

なにか　欲しがってる　みたいだ。
Nanika hoshigatteru mitai da.
something [he/she] wants it seems/looks like
"He looks like he wants something." (PL2)

- *sō ka* can also be a question ("Is that right?"), but here it expresses a sudden understanding/recognition: "Ahaa!/So that's it!/Oh, I see!"
- *o*, to mark *nanika* ("something") as the direct object of *hoshigatteru*, has been omitted.
- *hoshigatteru* is a contraction of *hoshigatte iru*, from *hoshigaru* ("show signs of wanting").
- *mitai da* after a verb implies "that's the way it appears." The word is not related to the *-tai* ending that expresses desire.

A

危ない	abunai	dangerous, p. 31-35
挙句の果てに	ageku no hate ni	ultimately/finally, p. 104
上げる	ageru	raise (v.), p. 141
愛人	aijin	lover, p. 69
相手	aite	opponent/companion, p. 49, 54
赤ちゃん	akachan	baby, p. 62
開ける	akeru	open, p. 93
秋	aki	fall/autumn, p. 30
諦める	akirameru	give up, p. 117
アメリカ	Amerika	USA, p. 86, 123
あなた	anata	you, p. 24, 45, 65, 74, 83, 146, 150
兄貴	aniki	older brother, p. 50
アパート	apāto	apartment, p. 60, 82
ありえない	arienai	impossible, p. 93
歩く	aruku	walk (v.), p. 128
汗	ase	sweat (n.), p. 51
頭	atama	head, p. 96
あたりまえ	atarimae	a matter of course, p. 48
あたし	atashi	I/me, p. 15, 74, 85, 89, 143, 154
熱い/暑い	atsui	hot, p. 44, 47
会う	au	meet, p. 135
合わせる	awaseru	unite, p. 102

B

バカ	baka	idiot/fool, p. 17, 47, 148
ばかり	bakari	only/all, p. 75, 89, 100, 132-137
バツ	batsu	fail/no good, p. 19
バツグン	batsugun	outstanding, p. 95
ベランダ	beranda	veranda/porch, p. 21
別に	betsu ni	not particularly, p. 123
ビール	biiru	beer, p. 78
ビックリする	bikkuri suru	be startled/surprised, p. 100
ビンボー	binbō	poverty, p. 41
僕	boku	I/me, p. 12, 44, 83, 104, 130, 137, 151, 152
防臭	bōshū	odor-resistant, p. 39
ボタン	botan	button, p. 43
部長	buchō	department chief, p. 101
ぶきみな	bukimi na	weird/eerie, p. 100
不器用な	bukiyō na	clumsy/awkward, p. 80
文化	bunka	culture, p. 86
武士	bushi	samurai/warrior, p. 104
ブス	busu	ugly woman (slang), p. 85
病院	byōin	hospital, p. 106

C

チャイナタウン	Chainataun	Chinatown, p. 65
ちゃんと	chanto	properly, p. 138
違う	chigau	different, p. 77, 88, 118
近づく	chikazuku	approach/draw near, p. 148
調子	chōshi	condition/shape, p. 61
ちょっと	chotto	a little/a bit, p. 16, 76, 101, 118, 140

D

お中元	o-chūgen	summer/mid-year gift, p. 105
だが	daga	but/however/still, p. 140
大事な	daiji na	valuable, p. 68
大丈夫	daijōbu	all right/OK, p. 66-71, 146
だいスキ	daisuki	like very much/love, p. 55
だから	dakara	because/so/therefore, p. 47, 81, 86, 94, 137
だけ	dake	only, p. 22, 80, 101, 153
駄犬	daken	mutt, p. 67
ダメ	dame	no good, p. 17, 25
誰	dare	who, p. 58, 84, 108
惰性	dasei	inertia, p. 121
出会う	deau	meet, p. 109
でかい	dekai	huge, p. 86, 100
電話	denwa	telephone, p. 55, 58
デッチあげる	detchiageru	make up/fabricate, p. 100
デザイナー	dezainā	designer, p. 113
どう	dō	how/what, p. 106
ドア	doa	door, p. 109
どく	doku	move/get out of the way, p. 56
同級生	dōkyūsei	classmate, p. 129
どうして	dōshite	why, p. 24, 117

E

衛星	eisei	satellite, p. 51
英雄	eiyū	hero, p. 40

F

深まる	fukamaru	become deeper/deepen, p. 134
不況	fukyō	recession, p. 41

G

学校	gakkō	school (n.), p. 27
額	gaku	(picture) frame, p. 58
頑張る	ganbaru	do one's best, p. 106, 145
玩具	gangu	toy (n.), p. 133
元祖	ganso	originator/founder, p. 149
ガラス	garasu	glass, p. 82
元気	genki	energy/vitality, p. 155
ゲテモノ	getemono	bizarre thing, p. 148
月面	getsumen	surface of the moon, p. 93
疑惑	giwaku	suspicion, p. 134
誤解する	gokai suru	misunderstand, p. 63
ゴルフ	gorufu	golf, p. 49
強盗	gōtō	robber, p. 27
具合	guai	condition, p. 109
軍事	gunji	military, p. 51
グローブ	gurōbu	glove, p. 115
行列	gyōretsu	parade/line, p. 134

H

ハゲル	hageru	become bald, p. 121
入る	hairu	enter, p. 58, 140
始める	hajimeru	begin/start, p. 127
初めて	hajimete	for the first time, p. 123
博士	hakase	professor/Dr.(title), p. 55, 96

The Vocabulary Summary is taken from material appearing in this book. It's not always possible to give the complete range of meanings for a word in this limited space, so our "definitions" are based on the usage of the word in a particular example.

ロクに	*roku ni*	sufficiently/well, p. 44, 75
旅費	*ryohi*	travel expenses, p. 77
旅行	*ryokō*	trip, p. 77
料亭	*ryōtei*	Japanese-style restaurant, p. 53

S

寂しい	*sabishii*	sad/lonely, p. 28
探す	*sagasu*	look for/seek, p. 26
最近	*saikin*	lately/recently, p. 87
最高	*saikō*	ultimate/best, p. 95
サイクリング	*saikuringu*	cycling, p. 86
最初	*saisho*	beginning, p. 27, 100
最低	*saitei*	lowest, p. 85
幸い	*saiwai*	fortunately, p. 122
さかん	*sakan*	lively/thriving, p. 129
先に	*saki ni*	before/ahead, p. 84, 143
算数	*sansū*	math, p. 38
せい	*sei*	fault, p. 74
政権	*seiken*	political power, p. 55
世界	*sekai*	world, p. 40
席	*seki*	seat, p. 14
責任	*sekinin*	responsibility, p. 119, 149
責任者	*sekininsha*	person in charge, p. 118
戦後	*sengo*	postwar, p. 123
先生	*sensei*	teacher/instructor, p. 54-55, 61
専属の	*senzoku no*	exclusive, p. 113
しゃべる	*shaberu*	talk/speak, p. 76
社長	*shachō*	company president, p. 56, 106, 141
写真	*shashin*	photo, p. 58, 154
試合	*shiai*	game/match, p. 127
しばらく	*shibaraku*	a while/moment, p. 122
仕事	*shigoto*	work/job, p. 12, 130, 151
しかし	*shikashi*	but, p. 58, 107
試験	*shiken*	test/exam, p. 27
しっかりする	*shikkari suru*	be strong/steady, p. 146
仕組む	*shikumu*	contrive/plan, p. 27
新聞	*shinbun*	newspaper, p. 107
進学する	*shingaku suru*	advance (in school), p. 61
信じがたい	*shinjigatai*	hard to believe, p. 51
心中	*shinjū*	double suicide, p. 104
親切な	*shinsetsu na*	kind/good, p. 14
知り合い	*shiriai*	acquaintance, p. 28, 67
知る	*shiru*	know, p. 54, 99
システム	*shisutemu*	system, p. 81
従う	*shitagau*	follow/accompany, p. 58
静かに	*shizuka ni*	quiet, p. 139
食欲	*shokuyoku*	appetite, p. 30
招待する	*shōtai suru*	invite (v.), p. 129
趣味	*shumi*	preference/taste, p. 148
取材	*shuzai*	news gathering, p. 111
荘	*-sō*	apartments/villa, p. 65
早熟な	*sōjuku na*	premature/precocious, p. 38
そっくり	*sokkuri*	exactly like, p. 76
ソナー	*sonā*	sonar, p. 145
そんなに	*sonna ni*	to that extent, p. 98, 118
そんなら	*sonnara*	in that case, p. 97
それとも	*soretomo*	or, p. 115
すべて	*subete*	all, p. 27, 119
姿	*sugata*	figure/shape, p. 46
スキー	*sukii*	ski, p. 89
スクープ	*sukūpu*	(news) scoop, p. 100
スピード	*supiido*	speed (n.), p. 82
すっぽかす	*suppokasu*	stand (someone) up, p. 89
すると	*suruto*	then, p. 116
進む	*susumu*	progress/advance (v.), p. 124

T

食べ物	*tabemono*	food, p. 78
食べる	*taberu*	eat, p. 61, 73, 128, 138
立場	*tachiba*	standpoint/position, p. 127
ただ	*tada*	merely, p. 118
他意	*tai*	ulterior motive, p. 115
大変な	*taihen na*	awful/serious, p. 58
大切な	*taisetsu na*	important, p. 59
大した	*taishita*	great/grand, p. 81
タイトル	*taitoru*	title, p. 113
たまたま	*tamatama*	by chance, p. 61
ためる	*tameru*	save/collect, p. 77
保つ	*tamotsu*	preserve/maintain, p. 105
頼む	*tanomu*	request/ask, p. 84, 105, 126
楽しむ	*tanoshimu*	enjoy, p. 84
確かに	*tashika ni*	indeed/for certain, p. 137
助かる	*tasukaru*	be helped, p. 105
立てる	*tateru*	uphold/prop up (v.), p. 103
立つ	*tatsu*	stand (v.), p. 104
手紙	*tegami*	letter, p. 53
手入れする	*teire suru*	take care of, p. 79
偵察	*teisatsu*	reconnaissance, p. 51
敵	*teki*	enemy, p. 123
適当な	*tekitō na*	suitable, p. 122
てっきり	*tekkiri*	beyond doubt, p. 88
点	*ten*	point, p. 69
店長	*tenchō*	store manager, p. 58
展開	*tenkai*	development, p. 127
手のべ麺	*tenobe-men*	hand-made noodles, p. 149
テレビ	*terebi*	TV, p. 81
飛び降りる	*tobi-oriru*	jump down, p. 148
届ける	*todokeru*	report/deliver, p. 91
時	*toki*	time (n.), p. 38, 47, 109
とこ	*toko*	place (n.), p. 26, 100, 121, 122
所	*tokoro*	place (n.), p. 120-125
ところで	*tokoro de*	by the way, p. 125
特別に	*tokubetsu ni*	specially, p. 103
特集	*tokushū*	special edition, p. 41
泊まる	*tomaru*	stay over, p. 51
とめる	*tomeru*	stop (v.), p. 67
友達	*tomodachi*	friend, p. 28, 64, 153
ともかく	*tomokaku*	at any rate, p. 123
とにかく	*tonikaku*	anyway, p. 59
とられる	*torareru*	get taken/lose, p. 35
取り合う	*toriau*	take heed of, p. 99
搭載する	*tōsai suru*	load (v.), p. 125
突進する	*tosshin suru*	dash/rush forward, p. 141

つば	*tsuba*	spit/saliva, p. 24
つぶれる	*tsubureru*	be crushed, p. 104
潰す	*tsubusu*	crush (*v.*), p. 103, 104
ついとる	*tsuitoru*	is attached, p. 81
使い物	*tsukaimono*	something useful, p. 80
捕まえる	*tsukamaeru*	catch (*v.*), p. 94, 122
疲れる	*tsukareru*	tire (*v.*), p. 128
つける	*tsukeru*	attach, p. 24, 97
付き合う	*tsukiau*	socialize with, p. 111
通勤	*tsūkin*	commuting, p. 39
着く	*tsuku*	arrive, p. 14
作る	*tsukuru*	make (*v.*), p. 69
つまらない	*tsumaranai*	trifling, p. 73
つまり	*tsumari*	that is/in other words, p. 23, 81
冷たい	*tsumetai*	cold, p. 47
突っ張る	*tsupparu*	push/insist, p. 107
面	*tsura*	face, p. 100
連れる	*tsureru*	take (someone) along, p. 112
釣る	*tsuru*	catch/fish (*v.*), p. 122
伝える	*tsutaeru*	convey/communicate, p. 71
伝わる	*tsutawaru*	be conveyed/transmitted, p. 73

U

うち	*uchi*	I/me, p. 47
打ち勝つ	*uchikatsu*	conquer/overcome, p. 41
うちに	*uchi ni*	within (a time span), p. 126
ウチの	*uchi no*	our, p. 106
動く	*ugoku*	move (*v.*), p. 33, 52
受ける	*ukeru*	receive, p. 14
うまい	*umai*	skillful/tasty, p. 21, 48, 53, 68
運転手	*untenshu*	driver, p. 59, 67
嬉しい	*ureshii*	happy/gratified, p. 135
うるさい	*urusai*	noisy, p. 37, 139
ウサギ	*usagi*	rabbit, p. 151
失う	*ushinau*	lose, p. 107
後ろ	*ushiro*	back/behind, p. 46
ウソ	*uso*	lie/falsehood, p. 137
疑る	*utaguru*	doubt/have doubts, p. 27
撃つ	*utsu*	shoot (*v.*), p. 92
打つ	*utsu*	transmit, p. 145
美しい	*utsukushii*	beautiful, p. 134

W

若い	*wakai*	young, p. 104
分かる	*wakaru*	understand, p. 17, 43, 46, 59, 80, 89, 106, 115, 116
わけ	*wake*	situation/reason, 69, 81, 114-119
我々	*wareware*	we/us, p. 33, 56, 123
悪い	*warui*	bad, p. 61, 109
わし	*washi*	I/me, p. 23
私	*watashi*	I/me, p. 45, 54, 55, 63, 69, 73, 76, 87, 93, 107, 116, 122, 134, 142
渡す	*watasu*	hand over, p. 83
技	*waza*	technique/move, p. 82

Y

やはり	*yahari*	really/after all, p. 25-30, 68
厄介払い	*yakkaibarai*	ridding of nuisance, p. 93
約束	*yakusoku*	promise (*n.*), p. 109
やましい	*yamashii*	shameful, p. 137
辞める	*yameru*	quit work/resign, p. 154
やっぱり	*yappari*	as expected/after all, p. 25-30, 60, 61
やる	*yaru*	do, p. 129, 151, 155
休み	*yasumi*	day off, p. 12, 130
やつ	*yatsu*	one/type/guy, p. 29, 80
やつら	*yatsura*	guys/people, p. 37
用意	*yōi*	preparation, p. 57
用事	*yōji*	business, p. 145
よけい	*yokei*	all the more, p. 111
予期する	*yoki suru*	expect/anticipate, p. 127
よこす	*yokosu*	hand over, p. 139
よく	*yoku*	much/often, p. 79
よく	*yoku*	well/effectively, p. 129
要求	*yōkyū*	demand (*n.*), p. 56
嫁	*yome*	bride, p. 153
読む	*yomu*	read, p. 49
夜	*yoru*	night, p. 44
容姿	*yōshi*	one's face & figure, p. 95
ゆび	*yubi*	finger, p. 40
郵便局	*yūbin-kyoku*	post office, p. 147
雪	*yuki*	snow (*n.*), p. 21
雪だるま	*yuki daruma*	snowman, p. 21
ゆっくり	*yukkuri*	slowly/leisurely, p. 110, 141
ゆるす	*yurusu*	forgive/excuse, p. 136
ゆずる	*yuzuru*	give up/yield, p. 14

Z

全部	*zenbu*	all/entirely, p. 107
俗物	*zokubutsu*	worldly/vulgar person, p. 143

Notes

Notes

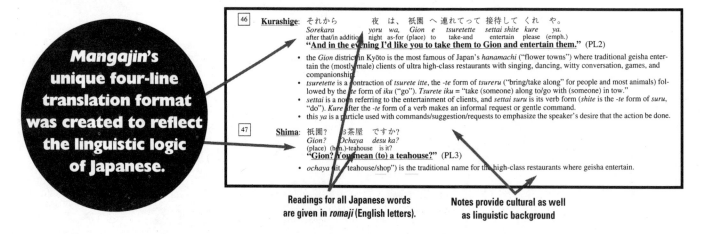

Mangajin gives you insights into what's going on in Japan...

Mangajin is more than just manga. Each issue our reporters give you insights into hot topics and current trends in Japan, like:

- Late-Night TV
- The Karaoke Craze
- Japan's Car Culture
- Eating on the Run
- Gambling in Japan

- Nomo Fever
- Japanese Beer Update
- Pachinko
- Sake Connoisseur's Guide
- Foreigners in Manga
- Japanese Pop Music
- Traveling in Japan
- Hit Products
- TV News in Japan

Mangajin brings you the latest on books, computers, and more...

Some of the world's sharpest Japan experts write in *Mangajin*, making it one of the best sources around for information on Japan.

Whether you use a Mac or PC, our computer reviews keep you up-to-date on the latest in Japanese language-learning software, and also help you keep your machine computing fluently in Japanese.

You'll find other features like book reviews, political cartoons, product news, language bloopers, information resources and a column on Japanese cuisine.

There are also classified and catalog sections which bring you a wide array of Japan-related products, services and opportunities.

Mangajin magazine is the home of the "Basic Japanese" column, source of the authentic Japanese manga examples used in *Basic Japanese Through Comics*.

Mangajin's manga pages are now available on cassette tape!

Audio reenactments of all of *Mangajin*'s manga pages are now available on cassette tapes.

Unlike many language-learning tapes which have a single speaker reading the lines in a monotone, *Mangajin*'s tapes feature voice actors who play out the parts and bring the manga stories to life.

Side "A" of the *Mangajin* tapes gives you each sentence or line of

Japanese followed by a pause for repeating, then the same line in English with a pause.

Side "B" provides the entire content of each story in Japanese, with no pauses, then the entire story in English with no pauses.

"The tapes make the story and the language come alive. I can check my reading with the speaking; it's helpful and fun."
—*Mangajin* tape subscriber

10 Issues: $39.95/¥8,300. Subscribe Today!

In the US: A one-year subscription to *Mangajin* (10 issues) is $39.95. A one-year subscription to *Mangajin* magazine which includes a tape with each issue is $119.95. US cover price is $5.50. Individual tape is $10.95.

In Japan: A one-year subscription to *Mangajin* (10 issues) is ¥8,300. A one-year subscription to *Mangajin* which includes a tape with each issue is ¥19,300. Japan cover price is ¥980. Individual tape is ¥1,200.

In the US: Mangajin • PO Box 7119 • Marietta, Ga. 30065 • Tel: 800-552-3206 • Fax: 770-590-0890 • email: orders@mangajin.com
In Japan: SSKC • Minami Aoyama 2-18-9 • Minato-ku • Tokyo 107 • Tel: 03-3479-4434 • Fax: 03-3479-5047

Need More Basic Japanese?

Get Mangajin's *Basic Japanese through Comics (Part 1)*

You hold in your hands *Basic Japanese Through Comics, Part 2*, a compilation of the Basic Japanese columns from *Mangajin* magazine issues No. 25–48.

The first book in this series, entitled simply *Basic Japanese Through Comics* (there was no *Part 1* in the title) is also available, providing you with a compilation of the Basic Japanese columns from *Mangajin* magazine issues No. 1–24.

Although the chapters in these books do not build on each other, and can be read or studied in any order, *Part 1* contains some truly classic expressions such as *Dōmo, Dōzo, Yoroshiku,* and *Desu.*

With the depth of understanding provided by *Basic Japanese Through Comics*, you can harness the full power of these words, and at the same time appreciate the subtleties of the Japanese language.

Learn essential expressions and get a slice-of-life look into Japanese society at the same time!

168 pgs. • 8.25" x 10.75"
ISBN: 0-9634335-4-7

Each chapter gives you six pages of illustrations from manga covering:

1. *Yoroshiku o-negai shimasu*
2. *Sumimasen*
3. Feminine Speech
4. Gaijin Bloopers
5. Hiragana, Katakana and Manga
6. *Ohayō & Omedetō Gozaimasu*
7. Creative Kanji Readings
8. *Dōmo*, The All-Purpose Word
9. *Dōzo*
10. *Baka*, the Basic Insult
11. *Shitsurei*
12. *Ii*, the "Good Word"
13. *Yatta!* The Exclamation
14. Saying Goodbye
15. The Concept of *Komaru*
16. Counters and Classifiers
17. Baby Talk
18. Informal Politeness
19. Introductions
20. "*–sama*" words
21. Hesitating with *Ano*
22. The Wide World of *Desu*
23. *Hai* (Part 1)
24. *Hai* (Part 2)

"…gives readers a window on …Japanese pop culture. Anyone who is serious about Japanese or modern Japan will want this book."
— James Fallows, Editor at the *Atlantic Monthly*; author of *Looking at the Sun*

"…a delightful volume that both educates and entertains. This is real Japanese as spoken by the natives."
— Glen Fukushima, Director, AT&T Japan, and former US trade negotiator

"…enjoyable material as well as valuable information on Japanese language and culture. I highly recommend it."
— Professor Akira Miura, U. of Wisconsin; author of *Japanese Words and Their Uses*

Only $14.95/¥2,500 in Japan

Available at your local bookstore or from…

In the US: Mangajin • PO Box 7119 • Marietta, Ga. 30065 • Tel: 800-552-3206 • Fax: 770-590-0890 • email: orders@mangajin.com
In Japan: SSKC • Minami Aoyama 2-18-9 • Minato-ku • Tokyo 107 • Tel: 03-3479-4434 • Fax: 03-3479-5047